YOUNG ABE LINCOLN

HIS TEENAGE YEARS IN INDIANA

---

*"I'll study and get ready
and some day my chance will come."*

By W. Fred Conway

Library of Congress Cataloging in Publication Data
Conway, W. Fred, Sr.

Young Abe Lincoln – His Teenage Years in Indiana
Library of Congress Catalog Number: 92-090038
ISBN 0-925165-09-3

FBH Publishers, P.O. Box 711, New Albany, IN 47151-0711
© W. Fred Conway, Sr. 1992

Printed in the United States of America

Front cover painting: *Boyhood of Lincoln* by Eastman Johnson (1824-1906)
    from the University of Michigan Museum of Art.
    Used by permission.

Back cover transparency: Courtesy of *Young Abe Lincoln Musical
    Outdoor Drama*, Lincoln City, Indiana

Typography and Layout: Pam Jones
Maps and Charts: Andy Markley
Cover Design: Ron Grunder
Principal Illustrator: Lloyd Ostendorf

Other Books By W. Fred Conway

- **Corydon — The Forgotten Battle Of The Civil War**
  Only two "Official" Civil War battles were fought on northern soil — Gettysburg, and ... Corydon. Includes the bizarre Ohio River crossing of 2,000 Rebels on captured steamboats.

- **The Most Incredible Prison Escape Of The Civil War**
  "The Thunderbolt of the Confederacy," General John Hunt Morgan, tunneled under the 4-foot-thick granite wall of the Ohio Penitentiary in an incredible and thrilling escape.

- **The Incredible Adventures of Daniel Boone's Kid Brother – SQUIRE**
  Squire's amazing exploits equalled or even exceeded those of his famous brother, whose life he saved in a dramatic perfectly-timed rescue.

- **Chemical Fire Engines**
  For half a century — 1872 to 1922 — chemical engines extinguished 80% of all fires in the United States. This fascinating history is the only book ever written about these extraordinary fire engines.

FBH Publishers
P.O. Box 711, New Albany, IN 47151
Phone 1-800-457-2400

"Here I grew up"

CONTENTS

INTRODUCTION

Abraham Lincoln and Indiana. To many, the two names are not synonymous, but well they should be, for as Lincoln himself said, **"Here I grew up."**

Lincoln lived in Indiana from 1816 to 1830 — from age seven to age twenty-one. Here, in the Hoosier state, he became acquainted with profound sorrow, grief, and death. Here he learned the dignity of hard work and how to overcome the problems of scratching out a living on the frontier.

Here Abraham Lincoln passed from childhood to adolescence and on into young manhood. Indiana was a free state during these transitional years in Abe's life; yet young Lincoln had the opportunity to befriend many slaves as he worked along beside them and played among them. He even enjoyed clog dancing with them. While he was a teenager on a trip down the Mississippi River, he witnessed his first slave auction. Abe said, "If I ever get a chance to hit that thing, I'll hit it hard."

It was here in Indiana that Abraham Lincoln's character, values, and virtues were formulated and forever ingrained into his heart and mind. Here he grew into a lanky six-foot-four, rail-splitting man. At age twenty-one, after spending fourteen years as a Hoosier, Lincoln crossed the Wabash River into Illinois on his way to greatness.

CHAPTER ONE

A NEW HOME IN INDIANA

When first my father settled here
Twas then the frontier line:
The panther's scream filled night with fear
And bears preyed on the swine.

— *Abraham Lincoln*

The year 1816 had been an unusual one not only for seven-year-old Abraham Lincoln, but for all the pioneers in central Kentucky. The coldest year ever on record, 1816 came to be known as "the year without a summer." Frost covered the ground in July, and the pioneers' crops failed. No one in America knew that massive volcanic eruptions on the opposite side of the world had spewed out so many millions of tons of ash that the sun's rays could not penetrate the earth's dust-laden atmosphere, so the weather remained bereft of the sun's usual warmth.

Four years earlier, another natural disaster had plagued these Kentucky pioneers. Suddenly, the ground beneath their feet began to tremble and shake as never before. So violently did it shake that a huge new lake was formed, and, for a time, the mighty Mississippi River flowed backwards.

Centered near New Madrid, Missouri, the most powerful earthquake on record caused church bells to ring as far as a thousand miles away in Boston, Massachusetts, as

7

Drawing by Ron Grunder

Seven-year-old Abe, his mother, and his sister, are saying goodbye to "Baby Tom," as they leave Kentucky for a new life in Indiana.

steeples were swayed by the undulating earth. The tremors continued for months, but little Abraham, just three years of age, was too young to remember this.

Whether it was the earthquake, the frigid weather with failed crops, the loss of landholdings because of fraudulent titles, aversion to slavery, just plain wanderlust, or even some combination of these factors, Abraham's father, Thomas Lincoln, issued a proclamation: the family would pack up and move away from Kentucky to a new state being formed across the Ohio River to the north. This new state was Indiana.

The Lincoln family left behind all their friends and many of their possessions in order to start life anew in a strange place. Seven-year-old Abe was understandably apprehensive because he knew not what the future held for him. His father's decision to move meant that Abraham Lincoln would grow from a child to manhood in Indiana. For fourteen formative years Abraham Lincoln was a Hoosier!

It was a cold and windy late November morning in 1816 when Abe, his mother, Nancy Hanks Lincoln, and his nine-year-old sister Sarah climbed Muldraugh Hill, which rose some 400 feet above the surrounding countryside, to the Redmond graveyard at the top. They had come to say goodbye to Abe's baby brother, Thomas Junior, who had lived only a few days after his birth during the year of the earthquake. Abe didn't remember him; he knew only that he had a little brother buried on top of the hill.

Quietly they stood at the head of Baby Tom's grave, marked only by a flat piece of limestone, which had the initials "T.L." chiseled into it. Nancy Lincoln knelt down and patted the little mound of clay, her tears falling onto the gravestone. But her tears, as fragile as her baby's life, were quickly dried by the wind. She was never to visit the grave

Nancy Hanks Lincoln, Abe's mother, often read to him and his sister Sarah from the Bible.

again, for within less than two years she, too, would join Baby Tom in death.

Nancy Lincoln was a loving mother, and she spent long hours with the son she adored, teaching him many things. She was a righteous woman, and she often read to him from the Bible. When he was five years old she taught him his letters, and when he was only seven, the year of the family's move to Indiana, he was already taking his turn in family Bible reading. He also was well-versed in writing and spelling by this age. In fact, young Abe was so precocious that he often amazed his neighbors, one of whom remarked, "He set everybody a-wonderin' to see how much he knowed, and he not more'n seven."

After the crops had failed due to the bizarre weather, Thomas Lincoln, alone, made an exploratory trip about 90 miles into Indiana, where land for settlers was less than three dollars an acre. He found a homesite that struck his fancy and marked it off by heaping piles of brush at the four corners. There he erected a lean-to where his cabin would later be built. He was a skilled woodsman and carpenter, and within two days, with the help of a man who offered him a job, the property was marked and the shelter completed. The land, 80 acres, was within Hurricane Township of Perry County.

When Thomas Lincoln returned to Kentucky, after little more than a week, he announced to his family that he had selected their homesite, that he had a job making casks for a distiller of brandy, and that they would leave at once. The Lincolns were not traditionally adventurers, explorers, Indian fighters, or hunters as were their distant relatives, the Boones.* They were tradesmen, farmers, and homesteaders seeking to improve their lot.

Abe, with his mother and sister, made his way down

---

* The exploits of Daniel and Squire Boone are chronicled by the author in his book, *"The Incredible Adventures of Daniel Boone's Kid Brother - SQUIRE."*

Drawing by Lloyd Ostendorf

"He set everybody a-wonderin' to see how much he knowed, and he not more'n seven."

Muldraugh Hill's steep and rocky trail. He crossed the turnpike at the bottom and got into the loaded wagon in front of their cabin where Thomas Lincoln was waiting. With little ado, the heavy wagon, pulled by horses, headed northward along Rolling Fork of Knob Creek and was soon out of sight of their cabin and Muldraugh Hill.

Periodically, Abe jumped out of the wagon and helped his father drive their hogs, which represented their winter's supply of meat. Inside the wagon were a feather bed with coverings, Nancy's spinning wheel, her cooking utensils, an axe, other implements, a steel plow point, and Thomas' carpenter tools. Also in the wagon was seed corn for spring planting, and tied behind was a cow for providing fresh milk.

As November turned into December in 1816, the Lincolns — Thomas, Nancy, Sarah, and Abraham — with their hogs, cow, and their wagon containing all the earthly possessions they hadn't left behind — came to a sight about which young Abraham had heard many stories. There it was — the majestic Ohio River, half a mile wide, and on the river was a huge boat which had two tall, smoke-belching stacks rising from its deck. Once in awhile it sent out a strange sound like a loud whistle. Seven-year-old Abraham stared in amazement at the wondrous sight.

The family had arrived at the ferry landing, operated by Hugh Thompson, opposite the mouth of the Anderson River where it emptied into the Ohio River on the Indiana side. Wagon, hogs, cow, and the four Lincolns boarded the ferry, and for about two dollars Hugh poled them across the river to Bates Landing.

They were now in Indiana, which only days before had become the nineteenth state to be admitted to the Union. In June, delegates had met at the village of Corydon*, some

---

* Corydon, Indiana's first state capital is described by the author in his book, "Corydon — The Forgotten Battle of the Civil War."

Drawing by Lloyd Ostendorf

Abraham Lincoln was on his way to a new life as a Hoosier.

forty miles east of the ferry landing, and had drawn up a constitution, which made slavery illegal in the state.

Once in Indiana, the hardest part of their journey lay ahead of the Lincolns, although it was only a stretch of another sixteen miles to their new homesite. The previous year the Perry County Court had ordered the road overseers to build a road twelve feet wide from the village of Troy (near Bates Landing) to "The Hurricane," with a completion date of November, 1816. If the overseers had carried out their orders, the road, passing within four miles of the Lincolns' homestead, would have just been completed. One of the Lincolns' new neighbors related that "Thomas Lincoln came in a horse wagon, cut his way to his farm felling trees as he went." Perhaps this was actually the final four miles.

The road followed an early trail to the village of Polk Patch*, which was situated some nine miles northwest of the Lincoln homestead, where a blockhouse had been built a few years previously.

Years later, Lincoln recalled that "I never passed through a harder experience than in going from Thompson's Ferry to my homesite." The forest was so thick with underbrush and grapevines that they had to hack their way through. They were stalked by panthers, who screamed at night. Bears grunted, wolves howled, and the hogs squealed, escaping from their hastily built pen. The Lincolns' first night on the Indiana frontier was fraught with strange sounds and dangers. Still several miles from their homesite, their experience was one of desperation. Thomas Lincoln stretched his arms toward heaven, and Abraham heard him say, " 'Tis the heavy hand of Providence laid upon me. Whom the Lord loveth He chasteneth." Inside the wagon, Abe, huddled next to his mother and sister, wondered if they would see the light of day.

---

* The author's wife, Betty Allen Conway, was born and raised at Selvin, Indiana, which originally was named Polk Patch — the same Polk Patch referred to here.

CHAPTER TWO

"LOVE, REVERENCE AND WORSHIP GOD"

A wild-bear chace, didst never see?
Then has thou lived in vain.
Thy richest bump of glorius glee,
Lies desert in thy brain.
—Abraham Lincoln

At sunup the pioneers continued their trek, hacking, cutting, and chopping their way through the thick under-brush, grapevines, trees, and saplings. By nightfall they finally arrived at the area generally known as the "Pigeon Creek Community" — a twenty-five square mile area that was home to the scattered cabins of twenty-seven hardy Hoosier pioneer families. The Lincolns would be the twenty-eighth family to join the community.

At the end of the journey was a cleared area just east of the forks of Buck Horn Creek, a small tributary of Pigeon Creek, where the wagon pulled to a stop at the lean-to, pole-house, half-faced camp, or hunter's camp, which were the various names by which these open shelters were known. Here was their new home — a three-sided shed of white oak and black cherry logs, which Tom Lincoln, with the help of brandy distiller Grigsby, a "close" neighbor who lived just two miles away, had built several weeks earlier. The shelter

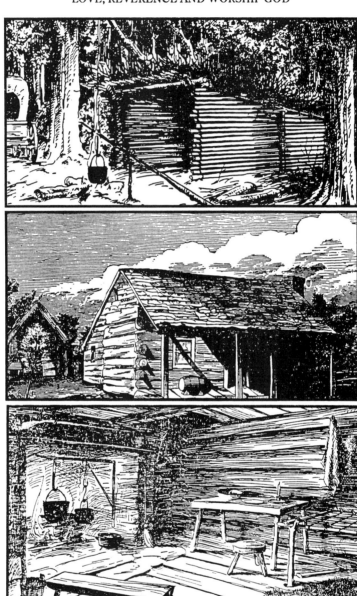

Drawings courtesy of Indiana Historical Bureau

Pole house; completed cabin; cabin interior

was twenty feet long and sixteen feet wide, with its southeast side completely open to the weather. And, this was the coldest winter on record in Indiana!

A stick and mud chimney took up most of the northwest back side. Tom Lincoln took a pair of heavy andirons out of the wagon, placed them on the tamped clay hearth, and with tinder, flint, and steel, set a pile of logs ablaze. The pole-house heated quickly, but it was only a temporary shelter intended to protect them during the few days it would take to build a real log cabin. Nancy brought in iron kettles and other cooking utensils from the wagon and cooked her first supper in their new home. As they prepared to eat, Tom Lincoln repeated the simple prayer he used at every meal, "Fit and prepare us for thy humble service, we beg for Christ's sake. Amen."

After supper Abe helped his father gather and carry in dry twigs which they spread across the clay floor of the shelter. Then, Nancy and Sarah spread bearskins and deer-skins over the twigs. Their beds were ready. Tired and sleepy, Abe had no trouble falling asleep as his mother prayed for their safety. He heard her say, "Remember our God is a prayer-hearing God."

As the sun rose, the Lincolns got a good look at their new home. The land was level and contained a growth of oak, hickory, and hazel. It was creek-bottom land. On the west side of the eighty acre tract was a good spring for drinking water, and on the south side a brook "ten links wide" gurgled its way in a northwesterly direction. The site of the new cabin would be on a knoll to keep it high and dry during periods of high water, and it would face the trail over which they had arrived.

Soon neighbors began to arrive to help the Lincolns build their new home. Thomas Lincoln was a skilled cabin

Drawing by Lloyd Ostendorf

Abe, still just seven years old, fells a tree for his new log cabin home.

builder, having built many of them in Kentucky. To illustrate just how fast a log cabin could be constructed, another family who had arrived in the same area during the same year left this record: "Arrived on Tuesday, cut logs for the cabin on Wednesday, raised the cabin on Thursday, clapboard put on Friday, and on Saturday made the furniture to go to house-keeping." With Tom Lincoln's skill as a cabin builder, and his expertise as a carpenter, one easily can assume that he and his neighbors had the Lincolns' new cabin read for occupancy within four days.

Thomas carefully selected the trees to be felled so as to provide logs a foot in diameter and twenty feet long. Sixteen logs this size were required for a house — eight for the back wall and eight more for the front. For the side walls, sixteen more logs were needed almost as long — eighteen feet. Shorter ones of various sizes were cut to fill the gables. In all, about forty, one-foot diameter logs were needed. Four large stones were placed at the corners for the foundation, and an axeman was stationed at each of the corners to notch the logs for a tight fit.

Clapboards, or wooden shingles, were cut with a froe to make the roof watertight. Openings for the door, window, and fireplace were cut out, and a stick chimney constructed on the outside of the cabin. Then the chinking began. Abraham and Sarah worked hard to help their parents build their new home. Abe split thin slabs of wood with his axe. He was physically mature and very strong for his almost eight years. He drove the thin slabs between the logs as high up as he could reach. Sarah daubed moist clay between the logs where the wedges left open places, completely sealing the cabin from the weather. They chinked and daubed both on the inside and outside of the cabin. Under the roof was a loft, and pegs were driven into the inside cabin wall to serve as a ladder to reach it. This loft room was Abe and Sarah's bedroom.

With the cabin made livable, Thomas Lincoln set about building a pole bedstead for himself and Nancy. The mattress for the bedstead was made of cornhusks and dried leaves. Nancy's feather bed, brought with them in the wagon, went on top of the bedstead and cornhusk mattress. Next, Tom made chairs, benches, a table, and later, a corner cupboard. To light the cabin at night, in addition to the logs blazing in the fireplace, there were candles and a lamp made by a wick placed in a cup of bear grease.

Drawing by Lloyd Ostendorf

Abe's father, Thomas Lincoln, and a neighbor notch logs at the corners for a tight fit.

Drawing by Lloyd Ostendorf

Abe climbed hickory pegs to get to the scuttle hole leading to his bedroom in the loft.

The cabin, fresh and clean, had the pleasant aroma of newly cut logs, coupled with the smell of the crackling logs in the fireplace. It was cozy, and it was *home.*

On December the sixteenth, another strong earthquake shook the area, which perhaps was a belated aftershock of the great earthquake four years earlier. But this one did no reported damage, so it was soon forgotten.

Tom Lincoln was now busy with his new job as a cask maker for Reuben Grigsby's applejack brandy — a favorite holiday beverage. This left the clearing of the land — the chopping and the grubbing of the undergrowth — to Abe, who at almost eight years of age was larger and stronger than most boys several years his senior. He already felt at ease with an axe in his hands. A few days after the earthquake, the Lincolns spent Christmas in the warmth and comfort of their Indiana home.

Over the holidays, there was plenty of time to write letters to relatives and friends back in Kentucky. But, Thomas Lincoln had never learned to write, and although Nancy Lincoln was an excellent reader, she never had learned to write either. Seven-year-old Abraham, however, accepted the challenge and very ably wrote letters to the folks in Kentucky. There was a biweekly mail route from Troy to Corydon, which continued on to Elizabethtown, Kentucky. Their new neighbors throughout the Little Pigeon community soon learned of the Lincoln boy's writing ability and persuaded him to write letters for them, too. He was marked as a gifted child.

In the evenings, Nancy Lincoln acted as a schoolmarm to Abe and Sarah. Their textbooks were the Bible and Dilworth's Speller. The latter even included some geography since it named the states and territories with their capitals. As well, it contained a section on poetry, which

Abe, using his father's rifle and shooting through a crack in the cabin wall, bags a wild turkey.

Drawing by Lloyd Ostendorf

young Abe loved to read over and over again. Among his other accomplishments, Abe became a poet.

Nancy read stories from the Bible to her children on a daily basis, and Abraham became thoroughly familiar with both the Old and New Testaments. His thirst for knowledge was incredible for a lad his age.

One of Abe's earliest memories of his Indiana home was the day, not long after they had moved into their new cabin, that a flock of wild turkeys appeared in the yard. Since his father was visiting the Grigsby's, Abe asked his mother if he could use his father's rifle to shoot one for dinner. With permission granted, Abe, taking the rifle from where it stood in the corner, aimed it through a crack in the wall and killed one of the turkeys. But rather than being elated at his marksmanship or the fact that the family would be eating a lot of turkey, Abe felt ashamed that he had killed such a magnificent bird. Never again in his life did he "pull a trigger on any larger game." One of his friends remarked, "Abe loved animals generally and treated them kindly."

But one animal was a real threat to the farmers. Bears took a heavy toll of livestock, and to diminish this threat community bear hunts were organized. Thomas Lincoln and his young son Abraham sometimes joined these bear hunts, which poet Abraham immortalized in verse that fortunately has been preserved.

> A wild-bear chace, dist never see?
>   Then hast thou lived in vain.
> Thy richest bump of glorious glee,
>   Lies desert in thy brain.
>
> When first my father settled here,
>   'Twas then the frontier line:
> The panther's scream, filled night with fear
>   And bears preyed on the swine.

But wo for Bruin's short lived fun,
  When rose the squealing cry;
Now man and horse, with dog and gun,
  For vengeance, at him fly.

A sound of danger strikes his ear;
  He gives the breeze a snuff:
Away he bounds, with little fear,
  And seeks the tangled rough.

On press his foes, and reach the ground,
  Where's left his half munched meal;
The dogs, in circles, scent around,
  And find his fresh made trail.

With instant cry, away they dash,
  And men as fast pursue;
O'er logs they leap, through water splash,
  And shout the brisk halloo.

Now to elude the eager pack,
  Bear shuns the open ground;
Th[r]ough matted vines, he shapes his track
  And runs it, round and round.

The tall fleet cur, with deep-mouthed voice,
  Now speeds him, as the wind;
While half-grown pup, and short-legged fice,
  Are yelping far behind.

And fresh recruits are dropping in
  To join the merry corps:
With yelp and yell,—a mingled din —
  The woods are in a roar.

And round, and round the chace now goes,
  The world's alive with fun;
Nick Carter's horse, his rider throws,
  And more, Hill drops his gun.

Now sorely pressed, bear glances back,
  And lolls his tired tongue;
When as, to force him from his track,
  An ambush on him sprung.

Across the glade he sweeps for flight,
  And fully is in view.
The dogs, new-fired, by the sight,
  Their cry, and speed, renew.

The foremost ones, now reach his rear.
  He turns, they dash away;
And circling now, the wrathful bear,
  They have him full at bay.

At top of speed, the horse-men come,
  All screaming in a row.
"Whoop! Take him Tiger. Seize him Drum."
  Bang, –bang–the rifles go.

And now a dinsome clamor rose,
  'Bout who should have his skin;
Who first draws blood, each hunter knows,
  This prize must always win.

But who did this, and how to trace
What's true from what's a lie,
Like lawyers, in a murder case
  They stoutly argufy.

Drawing by Lloyd Ostendorf

Aforesaid fice, of blustering mood,
  Behind, and quite forgot,
Just now emerging from the wood,
  Arrives upon the spot.

With grinning teeth, and up-turned hair —
  Brim full of spunk and wrath,
He growls, and seizes on dead bear,
  And shakes for life and death.

And swells as if his skin would tear,
  And growls and shakes again;
And swears, as plain as dog can swear,
  That he has won the skin.

Conceited whelp! we laugh at thee —
  Nor mind, that not a few
Of pompous, two-legged dogs there be,
  Conceited quite as you.

And furious now, the dogs he tears,
  And crushes in his ire.
Wheels right and left, and upward rears,
  With eyes of burning fire.

But leaders death is at this heart,
  Vain all the strength he plies.
And, spouting blood from every part,
  He reels, and sinks, and dies.

By the time the cold winter finally abated, Abe had turned eight. The hardy youngster was ready for a man's work, and with spring came planting time. Abe and his father hitched a yoke of oxen to their plow, and with Abe driving, they broke ground for their first crops in Indiana. In the prepared soil, they planted corn and flax. The crops were good, providing income which, when added to Tom's wages for making brandy casks, made the Lincolns have enough money to purchase an additional 80 acres, giving them a total of 160 acres for the family farm.

The letters Abe had written back to Kentucky produced a surprise. Soon to arrive to become their neighbors were Nancy's uncle and aunt, Tom and Elizabeth (Becky) Sparrow, and their eighteen-year-old foster son Dennis Hanks. Temporarily, they lived in the old pole-shelter where the Lincolns had first lived. Although Denny Hanks was ten years older than Abraham, the two soon became fast friends.

Abe worked hard during the days, clearing the land and working with the crops, but in the evening he read over and over from his books, which now numbered three. In addition to the Bible and Dilworth's Speller, he also had a copy of Aesop's Fables. Abe and his mother were very close. She helped him with the hard words and explained the morals of the fables. Soon he was composing his own fables.

The fourth book in Abe's library was *The Pilgrim's Progress*, which his father acquired from his brother, Josiah Lincoln, who lived near Corydon. Abe and his mother spent many long hours reading the adventures of Christian and his progress.

The fall of 1818 brought tragedy into young Abe's life — suddenly sorrow struck! Abe was nine years old when one of Thomas Lincoln's cows got the "trembles." Nothing could strike fear into a frontier community quite so much as a case of "milk sickness." It was a mysterious and fatal disease brought about by drinking the milk of cows that had the "trembles." No one knew a cure for the dreaded disease, and by the time the cow was found to be ill, it was often too late for those who had drunk its milk to avoid the sickness.

A writer in the Evansville *Journal* (Evansville, Indiana, is a city some 40 miles west of the Pigeon Creek Community) wrote about milk sickness:

> There is no announcement which strikes the members of a western community with so much dread as the report of a case of milk sickness. The uncertainty and mystery which envelopes its origin, and its fearful and terrible effects upon the victims, and the ruinous consequences upon the valuable property, which follows in its train, makes it in the eyes of the inhabitants of a district the worst looking for which can beset their neighborhood. No immigrant enters a region of southern Indiana, Illinois or western Kentucky to locate himself without first making the inquiry if the milk sickness was ever known there, and if he has any suspicions that the causes of the disease exist in the vegetable or mineral productions of the earth, he speedily quits it.
>
> I have passed many a deserted farm where the labors of the emigrant had prepared for himself and family a comfortable home, surrounded with an ample corn and wheat field, and inquired the reason of its abandonment and learned that the milk sickness had frightened away its tenants and depopulated the neighborhood. I saw this season a number of farms in Perry County, Indiana, lying uncultivated and the houses tenantless which last autumn were covered with corn fields whose gigantic and thrifty stalks overtopped a man's head on horseback.

The cause of milk sickness was this: a little white flower called snakeroot (actually the poisonous *espatorium urticae flyum*) thrived during a hot, moist summer, and cows ate the plants. The cows became sick, trembled, fell, and died. Persons who drank the cows' milk were destined to take to

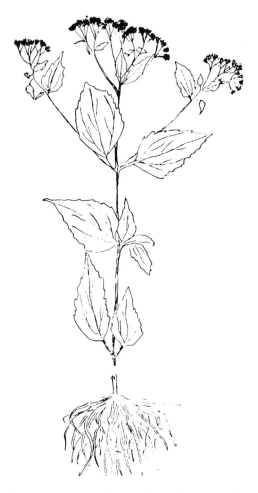

The poisonous snakeroot plant that caused milk sickness.

their beds, fall into a coma, and never awaken.

Nancy's Uncle Thomas Sparrow got the trembles and quickly made out his will, leaving everything to his wife Elizabeth. And if she did not survive him, their foster son Dennis Hanks was to become his heir. Before the will was several days old, Thomas Hanks was gone. Within a few more days, his wife Elizabeth joined him in death. Other neighbors became victims of the scourge, and Tom Lincoln was kept busy making coffins for them. Young Abe whittled the walnut pegs that held the coffins together.

Nancy Lincoln visited as many dying neighbors as she could to help out wherever possible. But after her neighbor, Mrs. Brooner was buried, thirty-five-year old Nancy Lincoln came home and went to bed because she, too, was ill. Abraham was called in from the field to hear his mother's last words to him. "I am going away from you and I shall not return," she told her grief-stricken nine-year-old son. "I know you will be a good boy. Be kind to Sarah and to your father. I want you to live as I have taught you and to love your Heavenly Father. Remember, our God is a prayer-hearing God. Love, reverence, and worship God." Soon the mother of Abraham Lincoln closed her eyes and joined Baby Tom in death.

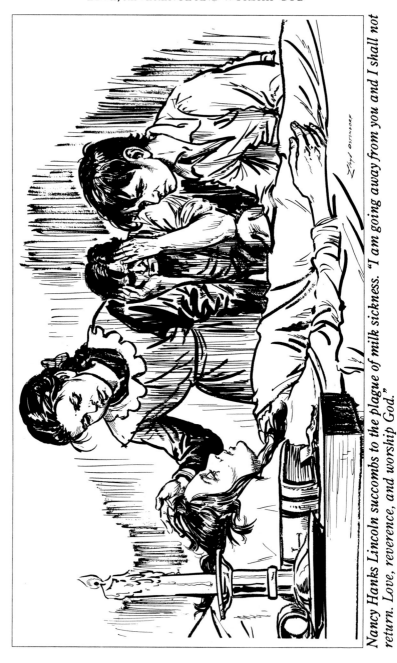

Nancy Hanks Lincoln succombs to the plague of milk sickness. "I am going away from you and I shall not return. Love, reverence, and worship God."

CHAPTER THREE

A NEW MOTHER

Abraham Lincoln
His hand and pen
He will be good
But God knows when

— *Abraham Lincoln*

While neighbor ladies washed and laid out Nancy Hanks Lincoln, Abe sat in the doorway of their log cabin with sobs racking his body. His father was busy building a coffin, and Abe knew he must whittle the pegs to hold it together. Somehow he did because it was the last thing he could do for his mother.

Neighbors placed Nancy in her coffin, and her husband, Thomas, using some of the pegs Abe had whittled, pegged down the lid. Reuben Grigsby was ready with his old mud sled, and gentle hands placed the walnut box on the sled to be drawn by the Lincolns' horse to the burial plot at the top of a hill, about a quarter mile south of the cabin, where the coffin was lowered into the ground. A son of Mrs. Brooner, whom Nancy had nursed and who had died the previous week, remembered, years later, that his father extended his hand to Thomas Lincoln at the graveside and said, "We are brothers now." He meant they were joined in grief, now that they both had lost their wives.

There was no minister in the Little Pigeon Community, but an elder of the Little Pigeon Baptist Church, Young Lamar, officiated as best he could. Just as Thomas Lincoln had placed a field stone on Baby Tom's grave in Kentucky six years earlier, so did he now place a flat stone on Nancy's grave into which he had chiseled "N.L."

Abraham felt his mother needed a real funeral, conducted by an ordained minister, so the nine-year-old boy wrote a letter to Reverend David Elkin, pastor of the Little Mount Church in Kentucky, where his mother had been a member before they had moved to Indiana. He asked Rev. Elkin to come and preach a service at his mother's grave. The kind Rev. Elkin, who had two sons living in Indiana, combined a visit to them with Abraham's request.

The belated funeral of Lincoln's mother. Nine-year-old Abe wrote a letter to a preacher in Kentucky to please come and preach a funeral for his mother.

A neighbor who attended the funeral service recalled the event as follows: "As the appointed day approached, notice was given the entire neighborhood. On a bright Sabbath morning the settlers gathered in. Some came in carts of the rudest construction, their wheels consisting of huge boles of forest trees, and the product of axe and auger; some came on horseback, two or three upon a horse, others came in wagons drawn by oxen, and still others came on foot. Taking his stand at the foot of the grave, Parson Elkin lifted his voice in prayer and sacred song and then preached a sermon. He spoke of the precious Christian woman who had gone, with the warm praise which she had deserved, and held her up as an example of true womanhood."

Another of her friends said, "She was a woman of deep religious feeling, of the most exemplary character, and most tenderly and affectionately devoted to her family. Her home indicated a degree of taste and a love of beauty exceptional in the wild settlement in which she lived." Another neighbor added, "She was a very smart, intelligent, and intellectual woman; she was naturally strong-minded; and a gentle, kind, and tender woman, a Christian of Baptist persuasion, she was a remarkable woman truly and indeed."

Still the plaudits continued. A member of the Grigsby family commented: "Mrs. Lincoln was a woman known for the extraordinary strength of her mind among the family and all who knew her. She was superior to her husband in every way. She was a brilliant woman, a woman of great good sense and morality. Thomas Lincoln and his wife were really happy in each others' presence, and loved one another."

Dennis Hanks, whose foster parents had died of the milk sickness a few days before the scourge had taken Nancy Lincoln, remembered her as follows: "She was 5'8" in height, spare made, affectionate — the most affectionate I ever saw — never knew her to be out of temper, and thought

© Lloyd Ostendorf

An idealized portrait of Nancy Hanks Lincoln by renown Lincoln artist and illustrator, Lloyd Ostendorf.

strong of. She seemed to be unmovably calm; she was keen, shrewd, smart, and I do say highly intellectual by nature. Her memory was acute, almost. She was spiritually and ideally inclined, not dull, not material, not heavy in thought, feeling or action. Her hair was dark, eyes were bluish-green — keen and loving. Her weight was one hundred thirty. She was one of the very best women in the whole race known for kindness, tenderness, charity, and love to the world. She always taught Abe goodness, kindness, read the Bible to him, taught him to read and to spell, taught him benevolence as well."

Clearly Abraham Lincoln's mother had been a jewel. By the time of her death, she already had mixed into her young son many of the ingredients needed to achieve greatness.

Eighteen-year-old Dennis Hanks, having lost both his parents, and having befriended Abe, moved into the Lincoln cabin. Eleven-year-old Sarah now assumed the role of housekeeper for her father, her brother, and for Dennis, who recalled Sarah trying her best not to miss her mother but being very sad: "Sairy was a little gal, only 'leven, and she'd git so lonesome missin' her mother, she'd set by the fire an' cry. Me 'n' Abe got 'er a baby coon an' a turtle, an' tried to get a fawn but we couldn't ketch any." Sarah did the best she could with the cooking, washing, and keeping the cabin clean. Four months after her mother's death she turned twelve, and two days later, on February 12, 1819, Abraham turned ten. Abe had a deep affection for his sister, and they often read the Bible and *The Pilgrims Progress* together.

A mile and a quarter south of the Lincoln's cabin was a new "horse mill" built by Noah Gordon, next to his cabin. Neighbors brought in their shelled corn and hitched their horse to the mill. By walking around in a circle, the horse

Drawing by Lloyd Ostendorf

"Sairy was a little gal, only 'leven, and she'd git so lonesome missin' her mother, she'd set by the fire and cry. Me 'n' Abe got 'er a baby coon 'an a turtle.

caused the burr stone of the mill to revolve and grind the corn into meal. The Noah Gordon mill was a popular place, with the settlers for miles around arriving not only to grind their corn, but to swap news and stories while they waited their turn at the grinding.

One late afternoon Abe and a new friend, David Turnham, who had recently moved into the neighborhood, rode the Lincolns' mare down to the mill, bringing a sack of corn to be ground. It was after sundown when Abe's turn came. He hitched up his mare to the mechanism and walked behind the animal as it poled the circular path. Wooden cog wheels turned the shaft that revolved the stone. Abe became dissatisfied with the slow steps the mare was taking, so he whacked her with a stick. Taking great exception to being hit, the mare let loose with a swift kick that landed on Abe's forehead, rendering him unconscious.

The bleeding, unconscious boy appeared to be dying,

"We tried to get 'er a fawn, but we couldn't ketch any."

Drawing by Lloyd Ostendorf

Abe at Noah Gordon's horse mill, where his horse kicked him in the head. "I was apparently killed for a time."

so his friend, David Turnham, made all haste to find Tom Lincoln. Tom drove as quickly as he could to the mill in a horse and wagon, all the while fearing that he had now lost his son as well as his wife. He picked up his seemingly lifeless boy, placed him in the wagon, and drove home. Neighbors soon flocked in to stay by his side during the night. Accounts vary as to whether it was a vigil at the bedside of a dying boy or a wake for a boy from whom life already had fled. But the next morning one of those near Abe shouted, "Look! He's coming back to life!" Another exclaimed, "He's coming straight back from the dead!" Abe's body jerked as he tried to talk. Suddenly, out came the words, obviously directed at the mare, "You old hussy!"

Upon his recovery, Abe recalled that, when she kicked him, he first had started to call the mare an old hussy because she was walking so slow. He greatly pondered, then, why he had completed his thought aloud after hours of having been in a coma. Finally young Abe arrived at an explanation that satisfied his searching mind: "Just before I struck the old mare, my will through the mind had set the muscles of my tongue to utter the expression, and when her heel came in contact with my head, the whole thing stopped half-cocked, as it were, and was fired off when mental energy or force returned. I was apparently killed for a time."

Not only was there a horse mill on Noah Gordon's property, a subscription school was established there the year Abe's mother died. A paper was passed around the Pigeon Creek Community, and patrons "subscribed to get a school." Tom Lincoln found the money to send both Abe and Sarah to the new school. The children's teacher was Andrew Crawford.

The school, a one-room building of hand-hewn logs, was sixteen feet wide by twenty-five feet long. It had a door,

Drawing by Lloyd Ostendorf

Abe and Sarah walk to their first day of school taught by Andrew Crawford.

a greased-paper window, split-log benches, and a stick-and-mud chimney for the fireplace. Outside was a cistern for drinking water. Above the door, pegged to the wall, was a fine pair of buck antlers for decoration; and hanging on the wall above Andrew Crawford's chair was a long, slender hickory limb, the traditional switch for errant pupils.

Andrew Crawford was a stickler for manners and etiquette. He had his pupils imagine that the school room was the drawing room in a fine mansion and that they were ladies and gentlemen. The thicket outside the schoolhouse was transformed, by imagination, into a formal garden. He taught each pupil how to make a formal entrance from the garden into the drawing room, where they were "formally" introduced. The girls tried not to giggle, lest the switch be used. But when they were presented to "Mr. Lincoln," they could not suppress their mirth.

Andrew Crawford often drilled his pupils with spelling bees, and on one occasion Katy Robey couldn't spell *defied*. She got stuck after the *d-e-f*. Abe winked at her to catch her attention and, then, pointed to his eye. Katy got the message and blurted out the *i-e-d*. "Abe was always ahead of all of the classes," fellow pupil Nathaniel Grigsby said of him.

The antlers mounted over the school room door were not high enough to be out of the reach of the tall Lincoln boy, who couldn't resist touching them. Then, one day when Mr. Crawford had left the room, Abe got up, took hold of the antlers, and tried to swing. A horn broke off, causing Abe to fall to the floor. Scared, he ran to his seat before Mr. Crawford returned. Abe knew a moment of panic when Mr. Crawford demanded, "Who broke that horn?" Abe looked sheepish but stayed quiet until asked, "Abraham, was it you?" "Yes sir," replied Abe. "I did it sir, but I didn't mean to. I just hung on it, and it broke." The teacher roared, "What did you hang on it for?" Replied Abe, "I wouldn't have hung on it, if I had known it was going to break."

Drawing by Lloyd Ostendorf

"I wouldn't have hung on it if I had known it was going to break."

Andrew Crawford often called upon his pupils to read aloud from the Bible, which was no problem for Abe who had been doing it for years. But one little fellow, remembered simply as "Bud," was not a good reader. When it came his turn, his verse to read was in the book of Daniel, which contained the names Shadrach, Meshach, and Abednego, whose names were included in subsequent verses as well. Abraham loved to tell the story of little Bud and the Bible verse:

> "Little Bud stumbled on Shadrach, floundered on Meshach, and went all to pieces on Abed-nego. Instantly the hand of the master dealt him a cuff on the side of the head and left him wailing and blubbering, as the next boy in line took up the reading. By the time the girl at the end of the line had finished her verse, Bud had subsided into sniffles and finally became quiet. His blunder and disgrace were forgotten by the others of the class until his turn was approaching to read again. Then, like a thunderclap out of a clear sky, he set up a wail which even alarmed the master, who with rather unusual gentleness inquired, "What's the matter now?"
>
> "Pointing with a shaking finger at the verse which a few moments later would fall to him to read, Bud managed to quaver out the answer: 'Look there marster,' he cried, 'there comes them same damn three fellers again.'"

When Abe's father, Thomas Lincoln, had first arrived in Elizabethtown, Kentucky, at age twenty, he had gone to work for an industrious man, Christopher Bush, who had six sons and three daughters. At the time, his daughter Sally was eight years old. During the first decade of the 1800's Sally grew up, and she and Thomas became friends. Tradition has it that they were sweethearts, although Thomas was ten years her senior. Then, one day while Thomas was on a flatboat trip down the Mississippi River to New Orleans with one of her brothers, in April of 1806, Sally up and married Daniel Johnston. When Thomas returned the first week of May, he bought her a wedding present. Not one to let any grass grow under his feet, a scant five or six weeks later found Thomas Lincoln married to Nancy Hanks.

Thomas got a wonderful wife in Nancy, but Sally Bush was less fortunate with Daniel Johnston. Within three months of their marriage, Daniel had borrowed money from Sally's brother who had gone to New Orleans with Tom Lincoln. Next, Daniel borrowed money from several Elizabethtown merchants. Within a year his taxes were delinquent, and he was sued by two of his lenders for non-payment of debts. A note on the court records stated, "Without funds." Next to his unpaid balance listed on the ledger of an Elizabethtown store was the anonymous notation, "An empty vessel makes the most noise." Obviously Sally Bush had married a ne'er-do-well.

Regardless of his lack of success, Daniel and Sally Bush Johnston were soon parents of three children. These children were destined to become the stepbrother and stepsisters of Abraham Lincoln. When Daniel Johnston died of unknown causes in 1816, two years before Nancy Hank's death, Sally Bush Johnston was left a penniless widow with three children. Undoubtedly, Thomas Lincoln, a widower with two children of his own in Indiana, learned that Sally's husband had died. So, in late November 1819, a year after his wife's death, Thomas Lincoln told Abe, Sarah, and Dennis that he had to make a trip back to Kentucky.

Promising to return soon, Thomas disappeared down the road toward the ferry landing. Ten-year-old Abraham, twelve-year-old Sarah, and Dennis Hanks were on their own until their father returned. He had not told them what his mission was in Kentucky; but, possibly to prepare them, he had told them of his dream. "I dreamed I rode through a path to a strange house," he related. "A woman was sitting at the fireside. I distinctly saw her features. She was peeling an apple." Mr. Lincoln took his best clothes with him, leaving Abe, Sarah, and Dennis wondering what he intended to do in Kentucky.

According to Sally's nephew, Squire Bush, who in later years recalled the incident, Tom arrived unannounced at Sally's cabin one day and informed her that he had been a widower for more than a year. "We have known each other for a long time and have both lost our partners. I want you to marry me," was his direct-to-the-point, if not eloquent, proposal. Sally replied that she could not because of her debts. Thomas immediately made a list of the debts, set out to pay each of them, and returned with a marriage bond. On December 2, 1819, the minister who lived next door pronounced Sally Bush Johnson, age thirty-one, and Thomas Lincoln, age forty-one, husband and wife.

Now, three years after his first move to Indiana with Nancy, Sarah, and Abe, Thomas Lincoln loaded another wagon. This time the wagon held the possessions of his long ago sweetheart, Sally. Into the wagon climbed Sally and her children: Elizabeth age nine, John D. age seven, and Matilda age five. All of them wondered, as had Abe and Sarah on Mr. Lincoln's first trip, just what the Hoosier state had in store for them.

Meanwhile Abe and Sarah longed for their father's return. Did he meet the woman in the dream — the one paring apples? Was there a chance she would come back with him?

51

CHAPTER FOUR

ABRAHAM ENTERS HIS TEENS

Abraham Lincoln is my name
And with my pen I wrote the same
I write in both haste and speed
And left it here for fools to read
                    — *Abraham Lincoln*

A large covered wagon, pulled by four horses, stopped in front of the Lincolns' cabin in early December, and out climbed Sally, the new Mrs. Thomas Lincoln, and her three children. Sally wasn't sitting calmly, "paring an apple" as Mr. Lincoln had dreamed, but she seemed pleased and eager to greet Abe and Sarah as they came running outside. Sally stood smiling at them as Thomas dismounted from the horse he was riding. Baldly, he announced, "This is your new mother, children."

Abe and Sarah greeted her politely, as they had been taught in their "formal introduction" classes at school. They saw she was about 5'11" — tall for a woman — had dark hair and seemed to be very friendly. But, Abe and Sarah were even more excited about their new stepbrother and stepsisters, whom they perceived would be their playmates. The small Lincoln cabin, about 360 square feet — only a third the size of today's smaller homes — now would have to house

"This is your new mother."

Sarah, Abe, and Dennis greet their new stepmother.

eight people: Thomas, his new wife Sally, Abraham, Sarah, Dennis Hanks, and the three Johnston children — Elizabeth, John D., and Matilda.

The children quickly made friends. Matilda later recalled, "My earliest recollection of Abe is playing, carrying water about one mile, and his pet cat that would follow him to the spring." With eight people crowded into the small cabin, Sally Lincoln needed to run a tight ship, and she did, in her friendly, easy-going, yet efficient way. Sally recalled, "When we landed in Indiana, Mr. Lincoln had erected a good log cabin, tolerably comfortable ... The country was wild and desolate." She persuaded Tom to replace doors and split shakes with better ones, and she carpeted the cabin floor with tanned deer skins. Dennis Hanks related, "She soaped, rubbed, and washed the children clean, so that they looked pretty, neat, well, and clean. She sewed and mended their clothes, and the children once more looked human as their own good mother left them."

Sarah Bush Lincoln was industrious, thoughtful, methodical, practical, and even-tempered. Like Abe's own mother, she was religious. Her pleasant ways soon won Abe's and Sarah's affection, and Abe said, "She proved to be a good and kind mother." There was gossip in the community that, before his wife's body was cold, he had remarried, taking to wife his old sweetheart who originally had turned down his marriage proposal. But the new Mrs. Lincoln paid no attention. Tom had waited over a year, his children needed a mother, and her children needed a father. Besides, it was none of the community busybodys' business!

When the new members of the family arrived, many things were carried in out of the wagon — a bureau, table, a set of chairs, a clothespress, bedclothes, kitchenware, and the most prized possessions of all according to Abe — four new books — *Webster's Speller,* the story of *Robinson Crusoe, The Arabian Nights,* and *Lessons in Elocution* by William Scott. Abe loved to read the new books in the evenings by the firelight until his father made him climb the pegs in the wall up to the loft, which he now shared with Dennis Hanks and John Johnston. One evening, as Abe read late into the night, Tom protested to Sally, "He's keeping us awake." Sally responded, "You leave Abe be. The boy is trying to study things out."

Drawing by Lloyd Ostendorf

"You leave Abe be. The boy is trying to study things out."

Webster's Speller, as *Dilworth's Speller,* contained much more than spelling. There was a section on "Precepts Concerning Social Relations" which included the relationships between various family members, such as reverence for parents, and even advice on choosing a life's companion. The last twelve pages of the speller were devoted to morals. Some of the questions and answers in this regard were as follows:

HUMILITY —Q. *What are the advantages of humility?* A. ... The humble man has few or no enemies. Every one loves him and is ready to do him good. ...

MERCY — Q. *Should not beasts as well as men be treated with mercy?* A. ...It is wrong to give needless pain even to a beast. ...

PEACE-MAKERS — Q. *Who are peace-makers?* A. ... All who endeavor to prevent quarrels and disputes among men; or to reconcile those who are separated by strife.

REVENGE — Q. *Is this justifiable?* A. ... Never, in any possible case. ...

JUSTICE — Q. *Is it always easy to know what is just?* A. ...where there is any difficulty in determining, consult the golden rule.

GENEROSITY — Q. *Is this a virtue?* A. ... To do justice, is well; but to do more than justice is still better, and may proceed from more noble motives.

AVARICE — Q. *Can an avaricious man be an honest man?* A. ... the lust for gain is almost always accompanied with a disposition to take mean and undue advantages of others.

FRUGALITY AND ECONOMY — Q. *How far does true economy extend?* A. ... To the saving of every thing which is not necessary to spend for comfort and convenience; and the keeping one's expenses within his income or earnings.

INDUSTRY — Q. *Is labor a curse or a blessing?* A. ... constant moderate labor is the greatest of blessings.

CHEERFULNESS — Q. *What are the effects of cheerfulness on ourselves?* A. ... Cheerfulness is a great preservative of health. ... We have no right to sacrifice our health by the indulgence of a gloomy state of mind. ...

Besides improving his moral beliefs, Abe's imagination must have worked overtime as he read *Robinson Crusoe* and pictured himself being cast up onto the beach of a lonely island as the only survivor of a shipwreck. Towards the end of the book, Crusoe is attacked by bears and over fifty wolves. Abe could easily relate to that scene. There were bears and wolves in the woods right outside his cabin door. The book quoted Scriptures and drew good moral applications from the adventures of Robinson Crusoe.

In *The Arabian Nights*, Abe most enjoyed "The Seven Voyages of Sinbad the Sailor," holding "Aladdin and his Wonderful Lamp" to be very exciting and unforgettable. Dennis Hanks teased Abe for reading *The Arabian Nights* and called it "a pack of lies." Abe replied, "Mighty fine lies." Dennis remembered that "Abe'd lay on his stommick by the fire, and read *(The Arabian Nights)* out loud to me 'n' Anty Sairy, an' we'd laugh when he did ... I reckon Abe read the book a dozen times an' knowed them yarns by heart."

Although the elocution book was not one of Abe's favorites, he read it many times through, and some historians consider that it was the most important book in his library.* The book dealt with the art of public speaking, and it included sections on gestures, speeches at school, acting in plays, and "rules for expressing with propriety the principal passions and humours which occur in reading or public speaking." Occasionally, Abe would disappear into the woods, mount a stump, and practice making speeches to the other children.

---

*The author considers the Holy Bible to be the most important book anyone can own. Perhaps Lincoln would agree.

Abe would disappear into the woods, mount a stump, and practice making speeches.

Drawing by Lloyd Ostendorf

This book even gave Abe an introduction to Shakespeare since it included excerpts from *Hamlet, Julius Caesar, Henry IV,* and others. It outlined the eight requirements for a polished speaker:

I. Let your articulation be Distinct and Deliberate.

II. Let your pronunciation be Bold and Forcible.

III. Acquire a compass and variety in the Height of your voice.

IV. Pronounce your words with propriety and elegance.

V. Pronounce every word consisting of more than one syllable with its proper accent.

VI. In every Sentence distinguish the more significant words by a natural, forcible and varied emphasis.

VII. Acquire a just variety of Pause and Cadence.

VIII. Accompany the Emotions and Passions which your words express by correspondent tone, looks, and gestures.

Abe's retention of everything he read was incredible. His stepmother said, "He could easily learn and long remember, and when he did learn anything he learned it well and thoroughly. What he learned he stored away in his memory, which was extremely good. What he learned and stored away was well defined in his own mind. He repeated it over and over again until it was defined and fixed permanently in his memory." Henry Brooner said, "For hours he would tell me what he had read." Another neighbor recalled, "While but a boy he had the best memory of any person I ever knew."

With the advent of fresh faces and personalities, it didn't take long for romance to blossom in the Lincoln cabin.

Thomas Lincoln set a good example for his young son. He was a man of great strength and courage.

On June 14, 1821, Dennis Hanks (who shared the cabin's loft with Abe and John Johnston) and Elizabeth Johnston (who shared the one-room downstairs with her mother, her step-father, her two sisters, and Sarah Lincoln) were married and moved into their own cabin about a mile to the east. Elizabeth was a child bride, only fourteen years old. Such early marriages were not uncommon in pioneer settlements.

With Dennis gone, Abe's sole male role model was his father, who always had set a good example for his son. Thomas Lincoln was a big man, about six feet in height, and he weighed nearly 200 pounds. Neighbors gave their impressions of him: "He was a man of great strength and courage, with not a bit of cowardice about him. His desire was to be on terms of amity and sociability with everybody. Thomas Lincoln was a man of good morals, good health, and exceedingly good humor. He had a great stock of anecdotes and professed a marvelous proclivity to entertain by spinning yarns and narrating his youthful experiences." One friend remembered him as "a good-humored man, a strong, brave man, a very stout man, loved fun, jokes, and equalled Abe in telling stories." One story Abe often heard his father tell was about the time Indians killed his father.

Abraham Lincoln had been named for another Abraham Lincoln — his grandfather. In May, 1786, Grandfather Abraham Lincoln took his seven-year-old son Thomas with him to a field outside the Hughs Station, a fort in Kentucky, where he was sewing hemp.* An Indian stalked him, shot him dead, grabbed up Thomas, and started to run. "Don't kill me," Thomas screamed. Tom's oldest brother, Mordecai, witnessing the attack from inside the fort, fired at the Indian and killed him. The Indian fell on top of Tom, who struggled free and ran for the fort. Just as Abe had lost his mother at age seven, Abe's father, at age seven, had lost his father.

---

*Today growing hemp or marijuana plants is illegal. The pioneers used the fibers of the plants to make rope.

Abe helped his father build the Little Pigeon Baptist Church, which the Lincoln family attended regularly.

One of Sally's relatives declared, "Thomas Lincoln was one of the best men that ever lived." Another in-law added, "Uncle Abe got his honesty and his clean notions of living and his kind heart from his father. Maybe the Hanks family was smarter, but some of them couldn't hold a candle to Grandfather (Thomas) Lincoln, when it came to morals."

Perhaps both his good morals and his superb carpentry skill were considered by the Little Pigeon Baptist Church building committee when they selected Thomas Lincoln to direct the construction of their first meetinghouse. Noah Gordon already had a horse mill and a school on his property — now he was to have a church — the first one in the Little Pigeon Creek Community. The building committee met with Thomas and gave him the plans:

"Build the walls of hewed logs in the following form to wit: The height one story and six feet, and the size twenty-four feet wide by thirty-two feet long with outlets in back and front of six feet square, three doors, five windows and covered with clapboards."

Thomas, assisted by Abe and others, not only built the log church — he built the pulpit, window casings, and other cabinet work. Abe, now twelve, enjoyed working next to his father in building a real church. After the church had been completed, Tom and Sally Lincoln became members, attesting to their acceptance of the Articles of Faith of the church as they appeared in the church's original minute book:

1. we believe in one god the Father the word & the holley gost who haith created all things that are created by the word of his power for his pleasure.

2. we believe the old & new testaments are the words of god thare are everry thing contained thare in nessarssary for mans Salvation & rule of faith and pracktice.

3. we belive in the fall of man in his public head & that he is incapable of recoverry unless restorred by Christ.

4. we believe in Election by grace given in Christ Jesus Before the world began & that God Cawls regenerates & Sanctifies all who are made meat for Glory by his special grace.

5. we believe the righteous will persevere throw grace to glory & none of them finely fawl away.

6. we belive in a general resurrection of the Just and unjust and the Joys of the righteious and the punishment of the wicked Eturnal.

7. we belive that good works are the fruits of Grace and follow after Justification.

8. we belive that babtism and the lord's supper are ordenances of Jesus Christ and that true belivers are the only proper subjects and the onely proper mode of babtism is immertion.

9. we belive the washing of feet is a command to be complide with when opportunity serves.

10. we belive it is our duty severally to seport the lord's table and that we orght to administer the lords supper at lest twise a year.

11. we belive that no minister ought to preach the gospel that is not called and sent of god and they are to be proven by hiering them & we allow of none to preach Amongst us but such as are well recomended And that we aurght to Contribute to him who Faithfully Laborers Amongst us in word and Docttrin According to our severrel abilities of our temporal [MS torn]. ...

The children of families which joined the church were not officially members until they came of age and made their own commitment. Abe never did officially join the Little Pigeon Baptist Church nor any other church. After he became President of the United States, his friend, Congressman Henry C. Deming, questioned him about his church affiliation. Deming recalled the conversation in later years:

"He said, he had never united himself to any church, because he found difficulty in giving his assent, without mental reservation to the long complicated statements of Christian doctrine, which characterize their Articles of Belief and Confession of Faith. 'When any church,' he continued, 'will inscribe over its altar, as its sole qualification for membership the Saviour's condensed statement of the substance of both law and Gospel, "Thou shalt love the Lord thy God with all thy heart, and with all thy soul and with all thy mind, and thy neighbor as thyself," that church will I join with all my heart and all my soul.' "

One day the wagon of a pioneer family broke down on the road near the Lincoln cabin. The ever hospitable Lincolns invited the family to cook their meals in the cabin while Tom set about helping them make repairs. There were two girls in the family, and Abe found himself taking a fancy to one of them. "I think it was the beginning of love with me," he later admitted. Abraham Lincoln the boy had become Abraham Lincoln the teenager, who found girls to be more than childhood friends.

CHAPTER FIVE

THE PRACTICAL JOKER

And when at length, tho drear and long,
Time soothed your fiercer woes,
How plaintively your mournful song
Upon the still night rose!

— *Abraham Lincoln*

After their wagon had been fixed, and the family had disappeared down the road, Abe began to daydream about the girl he had just met. He was smitten for the first time in his young life. So inspired was he by his feelings of love that his fantasies motivated him to write a romantic story — almost. He got as far as the outline:

"I thought I took my father's horse and followed the wagon, and finally I found it, and they were surprised to see me; and that night I put her on my horse, and we started off across the prairie. After several hours we came to a camp; and when we rode up we found it was the one we had left a few hours before, and we went in. The next night we tried again, and the same thing happened — the horse came back to the same place; and then we concluded that we ought not to elope. I stayed until I had persuaded her father to give her to me." But Abe never wrote the story, because he said, "It didn't amount to much."

Just as he dreamed about the girl in the covered wagon,

his step-sister Matilda evidently had romantic leanings toward Abe. One day he started through the woods on his way to chop firewood in a stand of timber on the edge of Pigeon Bottoms. Matilda's mother had forbidden her to go into the woods with Abe because falling trees and a sharp axe were too dangerous to be around. But, this day, Matilda couldn't resist following Abe. She quietly crept upon him until she was close enough to fling her body onto his back, throw her arms around his neck, and knock him to the ground.

The sharp axe her mother had warned her about proved dangerous indeed. When she landed, one of her ankles was cut badly on Abe's axe. Blood spurted and Matilda screamed. Abe calmed her down, tore a strip off his shirt and bound her wound. "What will you tell your mother?" he asked. "I'll tell her I cut my foot on the axe. That won't be a lie," Matilda replied. But Abe shook his head. "That won't be all the truth. Tildy, you tell the whole truth and trust your mother."

What Matilda told her mother, and how her mother reacted never were recorded. But Abe Lincoln always believed in telling the truth. Matilda was now age fifteen, and as Abe had no romantic interest in her, she allowed herself to be sparked by a neighbor boy, Squire Hall. Soon the romance turned into wedded bliss, and fifteen-year-old "Tildy" and Squire were married in the Lincoln cabin on September 14, 1826, with Reverend Young Lamar officiating. By this time, Young Lamar, the church elder who had spoken at Nancy Lincoln's grave, had become an ordained minister.

Young Abraham Lincoln was always industrious, looking for ways to earn some money. When he was thirteen, he learned from a traveler, who was passing by on the road near his cabin, that there was a great demand for gensing roots that grew wild in the woods. According to the nearest newspaper, published in Vincennes, "Chewing a root of gensing gives an uncommon warmth and vigor to the blood, and frisks the spirits beyond any cordial. It will even make old age amicable by rendering it lively." Abe knew where a good patch of gensing grew down near the place Matilda had cut her ankle. Inviting his pal Joe Gentry to join him and bring his grubbing hoe, Abe went down to the gensing patch and dug as much as 70¢ worth on some days — a considerable sum for two boys at that time.

The next year Abe got a job at the general store and meat market which opened in 1823 where the Boonville-Corydon road crossed the Rockport-Bloomington road. Abe's duties were to cut pork and render lard. The store was owned by William Jones, whose father, in violation of the Indiana State Constitution, openly sold slaves for a much as $400.00 each. This was Abe's first introduction to slavery, which he detested and vowed to fight against when he grew up.

Abe enjoyed working at the store, where he was able to swap news and stories with the folks who came to trade. Customers included "political fixers," escaped-slave hunters, story tellers, drunks, horse buyers, gamblers, and social reformers. Being there was quite an education for young Abe Lincoln. He often entertained customers with news he had read in the *Vincennes Sun,* jokes, and all manner of tales. Abe's winning personality was good for business, and Mr. Jones urged him to hang around the store even when he wasn't on duty. Dennis Hanks recalled that "Abe was warmly attached to Bill Jones." The store became an increasingly popular trading center, with Abe entertaining the customers. Folks came to the store from miles around for the express purpose of listening to the lanky teenage boy regale them with jokes and stories.

James Gentry, father of Abe's gensing-digging pal Joe,

noticed all the business conducted at Jones' store, and having plenty of money to invest, he decided to open a store of his own. Soon Jones had a competitor for the people's trade. Gentry's store also included a new post office. Jones' business was undiminished by the opening of a new store, however, which meant the wealthy Gentry didn't do as well as he had hoped. So, he bought Jones out and kept popular Abe Lincoln at the store, with Jones as manager. The community thrived, Gentry sold lots, and established Gentryville around his two stores. As Abe's stories and tales grew even bigger and taller, his following increased, and he began to take an interest in local, state, and national politics. To enhance his image, he often carried a cane which he had carved himself. "Abe is a well-posted politician," his employer, William Jones, proudly said of him.

Although James Gentry owned both stores, Jones' original store remained the more successful of the two. When someone asked Gentry what percentage of profit he was making on the sale of his goods, he replied, "God bless your soul, I don't know anything about your percent, but I know when I buy an article in Louisville for a dollar and sell it here in Gentryville for two dollars, I double my money every time!"

Gentryville grew and became a thriving community. John Baldwin, who had become Abe's friend, set up a blacksmith shop there. Peter Whittinghill* built a corn-cracker (grist mill) west of town. Gentry, not to be outdone, started a cotton gin, and Abe soon learned a new skill — cotton chopping.

Most teenage boys love to play practical jokes, and Abe was no exception. One day while he was clerking in the store, two fancy-dressed horse buyers from Kentucky walked in

*The author's wife is a great, great, great grandaughter of Peter Whittinghill.

and bragged that they were on their way north to buy horses. Abe left the store and quickly borrowed some tin pans and brass kettles from nearby housewives. They all knew Abe; he was everybody's friend. Abe ran north on the Rockport-Bloomington road with his pans and kettles and hid just past Saltzman's Hill. As the horse buyers approached, Abe dashed out of his hiding place clanging his pans and kettles and waving his arms. The horses the men were riding reared and refused to go on. The buyers, fearing a ghost or banshee had materialized, as Abe clanged the pans and yelled some more, turned around and headed back to Gentryville. They were never seen nor heard from again.

The following spring, Abe's father took him out of the store when it was time for spring planting. Now, Abe was not lazy, but his dad knew that plowing all day was more than Abe could take because he liked to read too well. So, Tom Lincoln attached bells to the yoke of the oxen that pulled Abe's plow through the cornfield. As long as Tom Lincoln heard the bells tinkling, he knew Abe was plowing. But it didn't take Abe long to figure out a way to keep the bells ringing while he read a book under a tree during the heat of the day. He simply turned the oxen loose to feed on the corn, and the bells kept tinkling.

Abe's pal, Joe Gentry, came out to see Abe at work and found him asleep under a walnut tree with a book in his hand. "Wake up, Abe!" he yelled as he shoved him. The oxen are eating the tops off your corn." Abe rubbed his eyes and offered, "Oh, that's all right, Joe. It'll grow out again." And it did. Alternating sunshine and rain made the corn grow so fast that Abe was sure he could hear the ears crackling. "The rain makes the corn laugh," he told Joe.

About a mile and a half north of the Lincoln cabin was the farm where pretty Elizabeth Wood lived with her family.

Abe loved to read too well to make a diligent farm worker. His search for knowlege was unending.

Abe's father took him out of the store when it was time for spring planting, but plowing all day was more than Abe could take.

Abe was determined to attract her attention; then, one day his chance came. His father had purchased an ox, named Buck, from Elizabeth's father, but the first night the ox stayed at the Lincoln farm, he got homesick, broke out, and found his way to his former home. Abe volunteered to go up to the Woods' to fetch Buck. When Abe arrived, Mr. Woods offered him a rope to lead the ox, but Abe declined, "I won't lead him. I'll ride that ox home and make him pay for his smartness," Abe declared.

Riding on the back of an ox promised to be quite a sight, so Elizabeth came out to watch. It was Abe's hour to show off, and he wasn't going to miss his opportunity. He waved "bye" to Elizabeth and then leaped onto Buck's back. Buck wouldn't budge. "Get out of here!" Abe yelled as he kicked the ox in the sides. Buck jumped into the air and came down running. He bucked as hard as he could in an effort to throw Abe off his back, but Abe stuck tight. As Elizabeth watched, Buck jumped the fence and disappeared down the road with Abe still hanging on for all he was worth. Abe rode him all the way home, where his father was working in the barnyard. Triumphant, Abe grinned and said, "I gentled him Pap."

Abe's pal, Joe Gentry, had an older brother Matthew who was known to be exceptionally bright and studious. But, one day in 1824, without warning, Matthew went out of his mind. Fifteen-year-old Abe was there when it happened. He was shocked to see the eighteen-year-old young man go beserk, scream, fight his father, attack his mother, and attempt to maim himself. It made a lasting impression on Abe, who composed a poem about the occurrence. Abe said, "In my poetizing mood I could not forget the impression his case made upon me." Only two stanzas of Abe's poem have been preserved:

And when at length, the drear and long,
  Time soothed your fiercer woes,
How plaintively your mournful song
  Upon the still night rose!

To drink its strains I've stole away
  All silently and still,
Ere yet the rising god of day
  Had streaked the Eastern hill.

The next year, when Abe had turned sixteen, his father, ordinarily thrifty and prudent, fell onto hard financial times because of his reluctance to say "no" to a neighbor in need. Tom Lincoln had co-signed a neighbor's note, which was coming due, and the man either couldn't or wouldn't make the payment. Tom Lincoln's soft heart had got him in trouble. Reluctantly, he had a talk with his sixteen-year-old son: "I've got it to pay, and it's going to sweep away just about everything we got unless I can hire you out." Abe, a dutiful and understanding son, didn't hesitate. "All right, hire me out," he quickly agreed.

Abe knew that Josiah "Cy" Crawford, who lived two miles south of the Lincoln's, was looking for a farmhand. Abe walked down to the Crawford place to offer his services. Cy hired Abe for twenty-five cents a day and had him build a new hog pen. He needed a stronger one because wolves and panthers had been getting into his pen and killing his hogs. Abe split heavy whiteoak rails, notched them, and fitted them together as he would have done in building a log cabin. Cy Crawford was pleased and kept Abe on to dig a new well. Cy became attached to the lanky, six-foot-tall teenager.

Sometimes the two would roughhouse, scuffle, and wrestle. Cy's wife Elizabeth said, "Sometimes Abe threw Cy and sometimes Cy threw Abe. They was always playing pranks on each other."

Abe finished the well, which was deep, cylindrical, and lined with limestone. Next, Cy sent him into the cornfield. Then, Cy hired Abe's sister Sarah to do housework, while Cy and his wife Elizabeth worked along side Abe in the cornfield. They often talked as they worked, and Elizabeth Crawford remembered Abe saying, "I don't always intend to delve, grub, shuck corn, split rails and the like." She added, "Abe worked hard and faithful. When he missed time he would not charge for it."

Seeing that both Abe and Sarah were making money working for Cy Crawford, Tom Lincoln soon joined his son and daughter in the Crawfords' employ. Tom was to build the Crawfords a new house. Abe acted as a sawyer, whipsawing the boards. He worked hard, still earning twenty-five cents a day to help his father meet the payments on his neighbor's note. Yet, in the evenings after supper, he had plenty of energy left to tease his sister Sarah and the two Crawford girls. He pulled their hair and played tricks on them until they ran from the room squealing.

One evening Abe's teasing became too much for Elizabeth Crawford to ignore, and she said, "Abe, you ought to be ashamed of yourself. What do you expect will become of you?" Abe instantly replied, "Be President of the United States." Mrs. Crawford scoffed, "You'd make a pretty President with all your tricks, now wouldn't you?" Abe, turning serious, offered, "I'll study and get ready and some day my chance will come."

CHAPTER SIX

AN INTEREST
IN GIRLS

This woman she was taken
From under Adam's arm
So she must be protected
From injuries and harm.

— Abraham Lincoln

Abraham Lincoln was somewhat of an entrepreneur at heart, as evidenced by his venture in digging and selling gensing. Now, in the summer of 1826, another opportunity for making money presented itself. More and more steamboats were plying the nearby Ohio River, and they needed fuel in the form of cordwood to keep their boilers fired. Sixteen-year-old Abe could cut cordwood with his axe as well and as fast any anyone in southern Indiana. To meet the increased demands for fuel for the steamboats, he formed a cordwood cutting team, consisting of himself, Dennis Hanks, and Matilda's new husband, Squire Hall.

They located their operation near the confluence of the Anderson and Ohio Rivers and were soon selling their wood for fifty cents a cord. But, for whatever reason, the business was of short duration. Seeing another opportunity for employment, young Abe became the captain of the ferry boat that crossed the Anderson River at the mouth of the Ohio. Soon, he was living at the home of James Taylor, who owned

Abe would row passengers in his small boat for 6¼¢ per trip.

Drawing by Lloyd Ostendorf

the ferry boat. While there, Abe shared a room with James' twelve-year-old son Green. Abe's salary was $6.00 a month.

When asked to recall her childhood memories in later years, an elderly woman remembered Abe operating the ferry when she was a little girl. She recalled his "gentle manner to the children, although the other pilot was very brusque."

If passengers on foot wished to cross the Anderson, Abe rowed them across in a small boat for 6¼¢ per trip, which was less expensive than running the ferry boat.

In later years, Green B. Taylor, the young man with whom Abe had shared a room, remembered an incident during Abe's ferry boat days: "It was during the season that Abe was operating the ferry across Anderson River for my father that we were told to go into the crib and husk corn; while we were husking the corn, Abe taunted me about a certain girl in Troy that I did not like and kept it up until I tore the husk off a big ear of corn and threw it at him. It struck him just above the eye, and this blow left a scar that Lincoln carried to his grave."

Through his ferrying, Abe saw a still greater opportunity for earning money, so he did some "moonlighting" on his own time. He built his own rowboat, which he made available at certain times to carry passengers out into the Ohio River so that they could board a packet or steamboat in mid-stream. On one of his first trips, he rowed two men out to a passing packet and saw them aboard. Much to his amazement and delight, they each tossed a silver half dollar into his boat. He had earned a whole dollar for a single trip!

However, trouble for Abe's new business was not long in coming. Two brothers on the Kentucky side of the Ohio River, John and Len Dill, had the exclusive rights to ferry passengers across the Ohio to the mouth of the Anderson.

Drawing by Lloyd Ostendorf

Two men who Abe rowed out into the Ohio River to catch a river packet each threw a silver half dollar into his homemade boat after they boarded the steamer.

Taking exception to Abe's new business, they filed a legal charge against Abe for encroaching upon their rights. They had him brought before a justice of the peace, who looked up the law. The law read, "If any person whatsoever shall, for reward, set any person over any river or creek, whereupon public ferries are appointed, he or she so offending shall forfeit and pay five pounds current money, for every such offence, one moiety to the ferry-keeper nearest the place where such offence shall be committed, the other moiety to the informer; and if such ferry-keeper informs, he shall have the whole penalty, to be recovered with costs."

It appeared that sixteen-year-old Abe was in plenty of trouble; but, acting as his own lawyer, he pleaded his case and presented evidence that his operation was limited to delivering his passengers to steamers in the *middle* of the river. He had never ferried any of them *all the way across* the river. The magistrate's ruling was "not guilty, inasmuch as there was no occasion cited on which he had set any person over any river or creek."

The ferry was less than a mile from Troy, a thriving village on the Ohio River bank. Abe often went into town to watch the boatmen, river pirates, gamblers, planters; and he even observed "ladies of the night" soliciting business around George Williams' tavern. Negro slaves were plentiful in Troy, and Abe learned to like them; they in return liked him. They even taught him to clog dance the way they did. According to Moss Emacoal, a neighbor of the Lincolns, "Abe got to be one of the best clog dancers in southern Indiana."

Abe got his boss, James Taylor, to let him off for a few days so that he could be home on August the second, a very important day, because this was to be his sister Sarah's wedding day!

Nine years previously, when the Lincolns had first arrived in Indiana in December, 1816, nine-year-old Sarah Lincoln and fifteen-year-old Aaron Grigsby had met at the spring, where they had each gone to fetch a pail of water. They immediately liked each other, and through the years their fondness grew. After Sarah had gone to work for the Crawfords, four-year-old Samuel Crawford spied on Sarah one evening when Aaron Grigsby came to call. Sarah, now eighteen, and Aaron had gone for a walk in the moonlight. Little Samuel reported to his mother, "I saw Aaron sparking Sally." (Sally was Sarah's nickname.) "I saw him kiss her." Elizabeth Crawford responded to her son, "Stop watching Sally and Aaron, or you won't get to go to their wedding."

Aaron was the oldest of Reuben Grigsby's seven sons. Now, Reuben, many noticed, had a strange way about him which few folks understood. But, Abe was always able to draw people out; so, one day he got Reuben to tell him his life's story. It seems that when Reuben was just four years old and his father was away from home, a band of sun-worshipping Indians broke into their house near Bardstown, Kentucky. To hide, Reuben scrambled up the stick-and-mud chimney, but the Indians found him and pulled him down. He watched as they killed his three older brothers and a sister. The Indians started north, carrying little Reuben and dragging his mother, who was holding her baby. When his mother couldn't keep up, they killed her, and then, dashed the baby against a tree until it was dead. When Reuben cried and became a burden to them, they threw him into the river to drown. However, an old Indian squaw swam out into the river to get him. The tribe let her keep Reuben. She became his foster mother and raised him as an Indian. For seven years, until he was eleven, Reuben Grigsby lived as an Indian. If Reuben told Abe what happened after that, Abe never recorded it nor repeated it. The Grigsbys were simply living in the Little Pigeon Creek Community when the Lincolns arrived.

While one of Reuben's younger sons, Nathaniel, and Abe became close friends, somehow Abe didn't completely trust the older son, Aaron, to take good care of his sister. He had misgivings about Aaron's marrying Sarah, for whom he had a deep affection. To commemorate the wedding, Abe put his poetic ability to work and wrote a poem which was read at the reception. Any of the wedding guests who listened closely to the words might have sensed a warning being given to Aaron, by means of Abe's verse.

As Adam was resting in slumber
  He lost a short rib from his side.
And when he awoke 'twas in wonder
  to see a most beautiful bride.

The Lord then was not willing
  The man should be alone
But caused a sleep upon him
  And took from him a bone.

This woman was not taken
  From Adam's feet we see
So he must not abuse her
  The meaning seems to be.

This woman she was taken
  From under Adam's arm
So she must be protected
  From injuries and harm.

Of course, Abe's friend, Nathaniel Grigsby, was at the wedding. He was now Sarah's brother-in-law. Nathaniel later said of her, "She was a woman of extraordinary mind. Her good-humored laugh, I can hear it now, is as fresh in my

mind as if it were yesterday." Sarah and Aaron started their married life together in their own cabin, and Abe wished them well and hoped for the best for his sister. With both Matilda Johnston and Sarah Lincoln now married, the family's cabin seemed empty.

Abe, older by now, found himself becoming aware of various girls in the Little Pigeon Creek Community. Polly Richardson claimed, "I was Abe's first sweetheart." She said that Abe took her to church, to spelling bees, and other neighborhood social gatherings. She further claimed, "Abe wanted me to marry him, but I refused." Her claims have been disputed as wishful thinking on her part.

Abe is reported to have courted Elizabeth Ray and to have given her a pair of earrings and a book. But Elizabeth married Aaron and Nathaniel Grigsby's brother, Reuben, Jr.

Abe used to walk Elizabeth Tully home from church. She claimed that she was his "first regular company" and that they kept company for several months. When asked if Abe had ever proposed to her, she answered, "No, but I could tell from his chat he wanted to marry me." But, she married someone else.

When Abe operated the ferry boat for James Taylor, he sometimes rowed across the Ohio River to call on Caroline Meeker who lived on the Kentucky side. But Caroline also married someone else.

Elizabeth Wood once said she was sure that Abraham wanted to become better acquainted with her, but she declined because of his "awkwardness and large feet." She married another.

Hannah Gentry was described as "a beauty noted for her amiable disposition, and her father was the richest man in the community." According to some of the neighbors, she would have become Mrs. Lincoln if Abraham had not been "too fond of onions, as she could not endure them." Hannah married another.

Sarah Lukens once told her friend, "I could a' been Abe Lincoln's wife if I'd wanted to, yes siree." Asked to elaborate, she replied, "Well, Abe tuk me home from church oncet." Some of the legends of Abe's teenage girlfriends may be more fancy than fact, but Abe himself told of falling in love with Julia Evans:

Drawing by Lloyd Ostendorf

Abe passed Julia Evans on the street at Princeton, Indiana. She bowed to him. "My heart was in a flutter. This was the scene of my first love."

"I passed on the street a very beautiful girl, the most bewildering creature it seems to me I had ever seen. My heart was in a flutter. The truth is I was so thoroughly captivated by the vision of maidenly beauty that I wanted to stop in Princeton forever." The young lady, who bowed to him on the street in Princeton, Indiana, where he had gone to have some wool carded, was Julia Evans, "admittedly the village belle." One of Abe's friends recalled Abe telling him, "This was the scene of my first love."

Still another of Abe's alleged romances was with Ann Roby. According to one account, she "described with self-evident pleasure the delightful experience of an evening's stroll down to the river with him, where they were wont to sit on the bank and watch the moon as it rose slowly over the neighboring hills. Dangling their youthful feet in the water, they gazed on the pale orb of night." But Ann Roby married Allen Gentry.

Drawing by Lloyd Ostendorf

89

Photograph courtesy of Young Abe Lincoln Musical Outdoor Drama,
Lincoln City, Indiana.

Abe and his friend Jefferson Ray on his first flatboat trip down
the Ohio to the Mississippi River.

After the wedding, Abe went back to running the ferry boat, but in his heart he longed for adventure. The many flatboats he saw being poled down the Ohio River held a fascination for him, and he dreamed of being on one. Abe, now seventeen, persuaded his father to let him take a flat boat full of produce — tobacco, corn, and potatoes from their farm — down the Ohio and Mississippi Rivers to Memphis or Natchez, where they would command premium prices from slave owners. His father, who needed the money badly, agreed. Abe knew that his friend, Jefferson Ray, was building a large flatboat on the Anderson River, so Abe struck a deal with him. Together they loaded their produce onto the new boat and poled out into the Ohio River. Abe was making his first of two trips down the river to the south — into slave country.

After the Ohio emptied into the Mississippi, they found ready customers for their produce on the shores of Arkansas and Tennessee. With their produce sold, Abe and Jeff took temporary jobs in Crittenden County, Arkansas Territory, chopping firewood for steamboats. Here Abe worked along-side Negro slaves, and as always, he liked them, and they liked him. They became friends.

Abe was back home in time for his eighteenth birthday. He gave his father a pocketful of bills and coins. True to his word, Abe had made considerable money to help pay off the debt the family had taken on to help a neighbor.

As soon as Abe returned, he asked about Sarah. Was she all right? Was Aaron treating her well? The answer came as a shock. Sarah was about to become a mother. In fact, she was in labor right then. Not only was she having a difficult labor, Aaron hadn't even got her a midwife, much less a doctor.

At their home, Aaron, finally realizing that Sarah was in trouble, bolted out of their cabin door and ran as fast as he could to get help. Sarah needed someone who knew what to do, and she needed him fast.

The only person Aaron could think of in his panic was his father. The Reuben Grigsby cabin was three-quarters of a mile to the southwest. Frantic, Aaron ran through the snow, reaching his father's home as quickly as the circumstances allowed. Once there, he and his father yoked a team of oxen to a sled and started back to get Sarah. They wrapped her in bear and deerskins, gently placed her in the sled, then made the return trip to Mr. Grigsby's cabin.

Still no midwife or doctor was available to help Sarah. The physician who usually treated the Lincolns, Dr. Edmund Moore, had moved away. Another doctor had been summoned, but when he arrived he was too drunk to be of any use. Finally, the local midwife, Mrs. Josiah Crawford, arrived, but she was not equal to the emergency she faced. Sarah's suffering kept intensifying.

Someone finally suggested that Dr. Davis from Warrick County be asked to come since Sarah's need was so great. Aaron's uncle William Barker went after him. Dr. Davis made the long trip, detouring around flooded Pigeon Creek, but by the time he arrived, Sarah was beyond his best efforts.

Aaron, not knowing what else to do, again took off running, this time to find Abe. He found him outside his cabin standing in the smokehouse doorway. Abe could tell from the frenzied look on Aaron's face that something was wrong. "What happened?" Abe asked. Aaron, ashamed, looked at the ground as he told Abe the awful truth, "Sarah just died."

A neighbor witnessed Aaron and Abe's confrontation at the smokehouse: "I will never forget that scene, Abe sat

Drawing by Lloyd Ostendorf

Aaron, ashamed, told Abe, "Sarah just died." Abe's body shook with sobs as he realized his sister was gone.

down in the door of the smokehouse and buried his face in his hands. The tears slowly trickled from between his bony fingers, and his gaunt frame shook with sobs. This was a hard blow to Abe, who always thought her death was due to neglect. They let her lay too long."

Sarah, with her stillborn baby boy in her arms, was laid to rest in the burying ground of the Little Pigeon Creek Baptist Church, which her father and brother had helped to build. A limestone slab carved with her initials marked the grave.* Sarah's death had a profound effect on Abe who suffered from periods of depression and despondency following her death. Sarah was not quite 21, and Abe was 19 when death separated them. They had been very close. The grief of losing first his mother, and now his sister, not only engulfed Abe in deep melancholy, but made him more sympathetic with others in their grief.

---

* Sarah's grave is now marked by a fine monument dedicated on May 30, 1916, which reads:

SARAH LINCOLN

WIFE OF AARON GRIGSBY

FEB. 10, 1807

JAN. 20, 1828

Two years later, in 1830, Aaron remarried, but within another year, in 1831, he himself was dead. He was buried next to Sarah. His tombstone is inscribed: "Farewell my friends, weep not for me, for we shall meet in eternity."

Sarah Lincoln Grigsby 1807-1828

"Her good-humored laugh, I can hear it now, as fresh in my mind as if it were yesterday."

CHAPTER SEVEN

THE SLAVE MARKET

On slavery: *If I ever get a chance to hit that thing, I'll hit it hard.*

—Abraham Lincoln

Later that year, Abe got a job offer which he took without hesitation. He was presented not only with a chance for adventure and the opportunity to learn new things, but a way to get away from the depression of Sarah's death which haunted him. Hers was a needless death, he felt, because of Aaron's neglect.

James Gentry, the wealthy store owner, intended to send a flatboat down the river to New Orleans. To accomplish this, he needed a stout hand to help oar the boat. He offered Abe eight dollars a month plus his passage back home by steamboat if he would take the job.

Gentry's son, Allen, who had married Ann Roby, had moved to the Spencer County seat of Rockport. He would be in charge of the trip. He already had been to New Orleans and back on a previous trip, oaring a Gentry flatboat, and he fired Abe with tales of the experiences he could expect to have there. The trip, indeed, proved to be the most exciting experience of Abe's life thus far.

Not only did Allen and Abe oar the boat all the way to New Orleans — first they built it! The flatboats of the period

Drawing by
Lloyd Ostendorf

With Abe working the forward sweeps and Allen Gentry handling the steering oar at the bow, the flatboat began the 1,222 mile trip to New Orleans.

were as long as 65 feet and as wide as 18 feet. The size of boat they built is unknown, but it was likely somewhat smaller. Allen and Abe spent several months completing it.

One evening, when the boat was nearly finished, Allen's wife Ann (who is considered by some historians to be one of Abe's first sweethearts) came down to the dock where her husband and Abe were working. Ann, in her later years, recalled the evening: "I said to Abe that the sun was going down. He said to me, 'That's not so; it don't really go down; it seems so. The earth turns from west to east and the revolution of the earth carries us under; we do the sinking, as you call it. The sun, as to us, is comparatively still; the sun's sinking is only an appearance.' I replied, 'Abe, what a fool you are!' I know now that I was the fool, not Lincoln."

In due time Allen and Abe completed the boat, and James Gentry had his hogs herded from Gentryville to Rockport, where Abe, an expert meatcutter, slaughtered them, packed the meat, and stowed it aboard, along with potatoes, kraut, hay, and ear corn. Just after Christmas of 1829, with Allen handling the steering oar at the stern and Abe working the forward sweeps near the bow, the loaded flatboat glided out into the Ohio River to begin the 1,222 mile journey to New Orleans. As they left, a cold winter wind buffeted them on the river, chilling them to the bone. They cooked their meals in the small cabin of the flatboat, and each slept there when it was not his turn to stay on watch. They were afraid to tie up at the bank at night lest the boat get frozen in the ice.

Several days after leaving Indiana, around New Year's Day, they entered the Mississippi River. Their trip took them past Real Foot Lake, which had been formed by the great earthquake of 1812, and on past the town of New Madrid, where the quake had been centered. Along the way, they

Drawing by Lloyd Ostendorf

Abe grabbed a handspike and knocked one of the pirates into the river.

100

began trading their cargo for cotton, tobacco, and sugar. On down the river they oared, past Memphis, Tennessee, and Vicksburg, Mississippi. Six miles below Baton Rouge, Louisiana, they anchored their flatboat for the night at the plantation of Madam Dunchene.

Exhausted from their day's work, Abe and Allen fell asleep. A feeling that all was not right awakened Abe, and he shouted, "Who's here?" There was no answer, but convinced something had disturbed his sleep, he jumped to his feet. As he stood up, several Negro slaves rushed at him from the darkness. Allen Gentry, awakened and alerted by the commotion, yelled, "Get the guns! Shoot 'em!"

Abe grabbed a handspike and knocked one man into the river, but three more leaped onto the boat. Allen met them, swinging a club. At last Abe and Allen, although outnumbered four or five to one, drove them off the boat, cut the cable, and cast off into the river. Only then did Abe discover the blood oozing from a cut above his right eye. The scar that resulted was a permanent reminder of his fight to save his life and his cargo from thieves.

Their attackers were runaway slaves turned murderers and bandits who intended to kill Abe and Allen, plunder the boat, and then sink it, leaving no trace. However, the slaves were not prepared for the strength they met in two young men used to chopping wood, plowing the ground, and oaring flatboats. Quick reflexes and finely honed muscles saved their lives and their goods.

When Abe and Allen reached New Orleans, they soon sold the remainder of their cargo, as well as the flatboat itself. Now, they were ready to see the sights of New Orleans. Abe had celebrated his twentieth birthday on the way down the Mississippi. Allen was two years older. They wandered through the city, which was built like an old French provin-

"If I ever get a chance to hit that thing, I'll hit it hard."

cial town, with narrow streets, and old fashioned houses. Lamps, suspended by chains that crisscrossed the road, lit the town. Most of the inhabitants spoke French, which Abe and Allen could not understand.

Meandering through the city, they came upon a crowd of people who were surrounding a raised platform. On the platform, Negroes were being sold into slavery. Because of his height, Abe could look over the top of the crowd to watch the proceedings. The sights he saw revolted him. Human

102

beings were being sold to the highest bidder, as if they were animals. Plantation owners were dispassionately and coldly buying field hands and household servants, who were bringing their sellers from $500.00 to $800.00 each. He kept watching as the auction progressed to the sale of "fancy girls." These girls brought from $1,500.00 to $2,500.00 each. They were not purchased to work in the fields, but were to be used for the purpose of gratifying the lusts of the rich plantation owners. It was at this point that Abe told Gentry, "Allen, that's a disgrace! If ever I get a lick at that thing, I'll hit it hard!"

Allen, realizing that Abe was seething with anger, and hoping to cool it before it boiled over, replied, "Abe, we'd better get out of here!"

Abe and Allen rented a room on the downtown side of St. Ann Street, and for two more days they took in the sights of New Orleans. They strolled past the American Theatre where the play *Richard III* was in progress, featuring Shakespearean actor Junius Brutus Booth, whose son, John Wilkes Booth, would become Lincoln's assassin three-and-one-half decades later.

After three days of sightseeing, the two men boarded a steamboat bound for Cincinnati. By the middle of March, they were docked at Rockport, back in Indiana. For three months of adventure, Abe had earned $24.00 and a scar over his eye that would always remind him of his trip to New Orleans, his fight with river pirates, and his first glimpse of a slave auction. All he had seen caused him to loathe and detest slavery. If only he might some day have an opportunity to fight against it, he was prepared to fight as hard as he could.

CHAPTER EIGHT

ON TO GREATNESS

I know there is a God and that
He hates injustice and slavery.
— *Abraham Lincoln*

Abe was now less that a year away from being his own man. When he turned twenty-one the next February, he would no longer have the obligation of giving his wages to his father, who was still making payments on his neighbor's note. Abe was obligated, however, to help his father with the debt for eleven more months. Unable to find work around his home, Abe struck out for Louisville, Kentucky, some seventy-five miles to the east.

In Louisville, he found a job in a tobacco warehouse at Fifth and Main Streets. One day, one of his co-workers (a white boy) accidentally knocked over a pitcher of drinking water and broke it. The son of the warehouse owner, hearing the crash, came around to investigate and saw the broken pitcher on the floor. He ran to his father's office, grabbed a blacksnake whip, and returned to mete out punishment to someone for having broken the company's pitcher. Without asking who had done the damage, he began flogging a nearby slave. "Don't do that!" yelled Abe. "He didn't do it. A boy came in here and broke your pitcher."

"Keep out of this or I'll give you some of it," the owner's

son retorted. When Abe stood his ground, the whip came down on him twice. It stung bad. Abe knocked the owner's son to the floor and smashed his fist into his bleeding face. Immediately he realized the trouble he would be in if he stayed, so he headed for the Ohio River a block away. His only hope for safety was to get across the river into Indiana. Quickly a mob formed to chase him, but the long-legged Abe outdistanced them, made it to the river bank, jumped into a skiff, and rowed out into the river for all he was worth.

The mob arrived on the bank too late, Abe had shoved off. Unable to reach him, the angered people threw rocks at him as he rowed toward Indiana. But, he dodged them and gained the Hoosier shore; then he fled into the woods. He realized that he had defended a slave and had struck a slave-holder's son — a grave offense. To avoid capture by his pursuers, he avoided the roads and made his way home through the Indiana wilderness, living on roots, berries, acorns, nuts, and wild honey.

Finally he arrived home in late summer, only to find the Little Pigeon Creek Community in the throes of another milk sickness plague, just like the one which had killed his mother. The summer had been extremely hot and wet, hence the wild snakeroot plants had thrived. Not since the scourge had taken his mother's life eleven years earlier had the vicious milk sickness struck the community.

Dennis Hanks expressed the family's concern when he said, "I was determined to leave and hunt a country where the milksick is not." Dennis' cousin, John Hanks, had already moved to Illinois. He wrote home to say there was plenty of good land to be had just waiting for a plow. Tom Lincoln, having lost his first wife to milk sickness, was not about to stay and take a chance on losing his second wife. "We're pulling out," he told Abe.

Abe helped his father build three covered wagons, one for themselves, one for the Hankses, and the third one for the Halls. All three families planned to pull out together. Preparations for the move had taken several months. Abe was now twenty-one years of age. On February 28, 1830, the Lincolns' wagon was loaded and ready to pull out the next morning. Three beds, the bureau, table and chairs, clothes closet, cooking utensils, andirons, tools — everything the Lincolns owned — was packed into the wagon.

Before leaving Indiana, Abe had two things he wanted to do. With his entrepreneurial spirit still intact, he went to the Jones store and bought, on credit, goods which he intended to peddle at a profit on the way to Illinois. The items he chose included needles, thread, knives, forks, necklaces, breast pins, and pocketbooks. The bill came to $36.00. Customers in the store questioned Jones' willingness to extend Abe so much credit since he was moving away. "I am satisfied," Jones replied. "Abe is honest. He'll make a great man one of these days."

On the morning of March first, Tom Lincoln was ready to pull out, but Abe was nowhere to be seen. His father was set to leave without him, realizing Abe would catch up later, when he saw Abe coming down the hillside. His eyes were red, and undried tears clung to his face. He had been at his mother's grave telling her goodbye. He and his mother had said goodbye to Baby Tom fourteen years earlier; now Abe, alone, was saying goodbye to his mother. Years later, while in the White House, he said of her, "All that I am or hope to be, I owe to my angel mother."

The three-wagon caravan, containing thirteen people, pulled out. The occupants of the wagons were: Thomas Lincoln, 54; Sarah Bush Lincoln, 41; Abraham Lincoln, 21; John D. Johnston, 14; Dennis Hanks, 31; his wife, Elizabeth

Drawing by Lloyd Ostendorf

Elihu Stout, Editor of the Western Sun, *explains the operation of the printing press to Abe, who soon begins to actually print the newspaper.*

Johnston Hanks, 23; their four children, Sarah Jane, Nancy Ann, Harriet, and John Talbott, all under 9; Squire Hall and his wife, Matilda Johnston Hall, 19; and their three-year-old son John.

Many of their friends and neighbors, as was the custom, went a Biblical day's journey with them. They included the Gentrys, Grigsbys, Joneses, Brooners, Lamars, Whittinghills, and Turnhams. David Turnham, who had

108

been Abe's friend for eleven years, said, "I never knew anything dishonorable of him."

On March seventh, they reached the town of Vincennes, Indiana, on the banks of the Wabash. They camped near the office of the *Western Sun* newspaper, which Abe had often read at Jones' store over the years. Curious to see the home of the newspaper that he had enjoyed so much, Abe entered the office. The editor, Elihu Stout, was setting type in preparation for printing the next issue, so Abe, seeing a chance to befriend him, asked if he could help him operate the hand press. Soon Stout stepped aside, and Abe, his strong hand grasping the lever, began to operate the press. Abraham Lincoln was actually printing the *Western Sun!*

The next day, March eighth, the caravan boarded Haines' ferry and crossed the Wabash River from Indiana into Illinois. Abraham Lincoln's life as a Hoosier had come to a close.

While working for Josiah Crawford, Abe had vowed, "I will study and get ready, and some day my chance will come." In Illinois, Abe was to say, "I know there is a God and that He hates injustice and slavery. I see the storm coming, and I know that He has a hand in it. If He has a place and work for me — and I think He has — I believe I am ready."

Photograph courtesy of Young Abe Lincoln Musical Outdoor Drama,
Lincoln City, Indiana

"If He has a place and work for me — and I think He has — I believe I am ready."

EPILOGUE

Lincoln ca 1844 at age 35 when he returned for his only visit to Indiana, the land of his youth. While on this visit, he was moved to write his most famous poem, My Childhood Home.

"In the fall of 1844, thinking I might aid some to carry the State of Indiana for Mr. Clay, I went into the neighborhood in that State in which I was raised, where my mother and only sister were buried, and from which I had been absent about fifteen years. That part of the country is, within itself, as unpoetical as any spot of the earth; but still seeing it and its object and inhabitants aroused feelings in me which were certainly poetry; though whether my expression of these feelings is poetry is quite another question."

Drawing by Lloyd Ostendorf

MY CHILDHOOD HOME

My childhood's home I see again,
  And sadden with the view;
And still, as memory crowds my brain,
  There's pleasure in it too.

O Memory! thou midway world
  'Twixt earth and paradise,
Where things decayed and loved ones lost
  In dreamy shadows rise,

And, freed from all that's earthly vile,
  Seem hallowed, pure, and bright,
Like scenes in some enchanted isle
  All bathed in liquid light.

As dusky mountains please the eye
  When twilight chases day;
As bugle-notes that, passing by,
  In distance die away;

As leaving some grand waterfall,
  We, lingering, list its roar—
So memory will hallow all
  We've known, but know no more.

Drawing by Lloyd Ostendorf

Near twenty years have passed away
   Since here I bid farewell
To woods and fields, and scenes of play,
   And playmates loved so well.

EPILOGUE

Where many were, but few remain
   Of old familiar things;
But seeing them, to mind again
   The lost and absent brings.

The friends I left that parting day,
   How changed, as time has sped!
Young childhood grown, strong manhood gray,
   And half of all are dead.

I hear the loved survivors tell
   How nought from death could save,
Till every sound appears a knell,
   And every spot a grave.

I range the fields with pensive tread,
   And pace the hollow rooms,
And feel (companion of the dead)
   I'm living in the tombs.

And now away to seek some scene
   Less painful than the last —
With less of horror mingled in
   The present and the past.

The very spot where grew the bread
   That formed my bones, I see.
How strange, old field, on thee to tread,
   And feel I'm part of thee!

Sketch of Lincoln cabin by John H. Rowbottom.

Appendix A

Persons Living in the 360 square foot
Lincoln Pioneer Log Cabin.

Dates	No. of Persons in Cabin	Names	Comments
December 1816 to Fall 1817	4	Thomas Lincoln, his wife, Nancy Hanks Lincoln; their children Abraham and Sarah.	Abraham and Sarah climb pegs in the wall to their beds in the loft.
Fall 1817 to October 1818	5	Dennis Hanks joins the four Lincolns in the cabin.	Dennis Hanks was a relative of Nancy Hanks Lincoln.
October 1818 to December 1819	4	Missing is Nancy Hanks Lincoln, who has died of the milk sickness.	Eleven-year-old Sarah takes over her mother's duties in the cabin.
December 1819 to June 1821	8	Thomas Lincoln remarries to Sarah "Sally" Bush Johnston, and becomes the step-father of her three children, Matilda, John D., and Elizabeth.	There are now eight persons living in the tiny cabin.
June 1821 to August 1826	6	Dennis Hanks and Elizabeth Johnston marry and move into their own cabin.	Elizabeth Johnston is a child bride at age 14. Dennis is 21.
August 1826 to September 1826	5	Sarah Lincoln marries Aaron Grigsby and they move into their own cabin.	Sarah is 19, and Aaron is 25.
September 1826 to March 1830	4	Matilda Johnston marries Squire Hall and moves into the Dennis Hanks cabin. Remaining in the Lincoln cabin are Thomas Lincoln, Sally Bush Lincoln, Abraham Lincoln, and John D. Johnston.	Matilda Johnston marries at age 15. On March 1, 1830, the Lincolns sell their farm and cabin and move to Illinois.

Appendix A
Abraham Lincoln's Genealogy

Lincoln's great-great-great-great grandfather	**Samuel Lincoln** 1619-1690	Born in Hingham, England. Came to America in 1633 as one of the six original settlers of Hingham, Mass.
Lincoln's great-great-great grandfather	**Mordecai Lincoln, Sr.** 1657-1727	Stayed in Massachusetts. Lived at Scituate in a substantial colonial home.
Lincoln's great-great grandfather	**Mordecai Lincoln, Jr.** 1686-1736	Born in Massachusetts. Married in New Jersey. Died in Pennsylvania.
Lincoln's great grandfather	**John Lincoln** 1716-1788	Born in New Jersey, married in Pennsylvania, lived in the Yadkin Valley of North Carolina where he was a neighbor of Daniel and Squire Boone. He came through the Cumberland Gap with them.
Lincoln's grandfather	**Abraham Lincoln** 1744-1786	Born in Pennsylvania, married in Virginia, killed by Indians in Kentucky when his son, Thomas, was age seven.
Lincoln's father	**Thomas Lincoln** 1776-1851	Born in Virginia. Married in Kentucky. Lived in Indiana. Died in Illinois.
	Abraham Lincoln 1809-1865	Born in Kentucky. Lived in Indiana and Illinois. Assassinated in Washington, D.C.

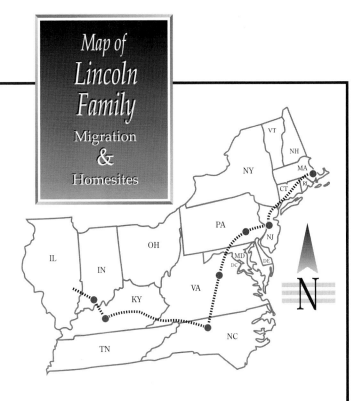

The States as of 1816, with the dates of their entrance into the Union

(Louisiana, Admitted April 30, 1812, is not shown)

1. Delaware, December 7, 1787
2. Pennsylvania, December 12, 1787
3. New Jersey, December 18, 1787
4. Georgia, January 2, 1788
5. Connecticut, January 9, 1788
6. Massachusetts, February 6, 1788
7. Maryland, April 28, 1788
8. South Carolina, May 23, 1788
9. New Hampshire, June 21, 1788
10. Virginia, June 26, 1788

11. New York, July 26, 1788
12. North Carolina, November 21, 1789
13. Rhode Island, May 29, 1790
14. Vermont, March 4, 1791
15. Kentucky, June 1, 1792
16. Tennessee, June 1, 1792
17. Ohio, June 1, 1796
18. Louisiana, April 30, 1812
19. Indiana, December 11, 1816

Map: Andy Markley

Home Sites
of Lincoln Neighbors

2. Dennis Hanks
3. Thomas Barret
4. Thomas Turnham
5. William Whitman
6. Thomas Carter
7. John Carter
8. Luther Greathouse
9. David Casebier
10. John Jones
11. William Wood
12. Peter Whittinghill
13. James Gentry
14. John Romine
15. Samuel Howell
16. Noah Gordon
17. Joseph Wright
18. William Wright
19. Moses Randall
20. Peter Brooner
21. Amos Richardson
22. David Edwards
23. Reuben Grigsby
24. Aaron Grigsby
25. Josiah Crawford
26. William Barker
27. Henry Gunterman
28. Benoni Hardin

Little Pigeon Community

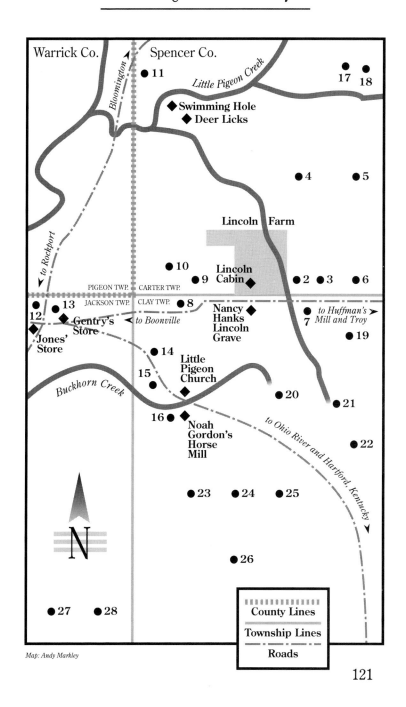

Warrick Co.   Spencer Co.

Bloomington

● 11

Little Pigeon Creek

17 ●   ● 18

◆ **Swimming Hole**
◆ **Deer Licks**

● 4   ● 5

to Rockport

Lincoln   Farm

● 10
● 9   **Lincoln Cabin** ◆   ● 2   ● 3   ● 6

PIGEON TWP.   CARTER TWP.

JACKSON TWP.   CLAY TWP.   ● 8

● 13   **Nancy** ◆   *to Huffman's* ➤
12 ●   ◆   **Hanks**   *Mill and Troy*
◆ **Gentry's**   ◄ *to Boonville*   **Lincoln**   7
Jones' **Store**   **Grave**   ● 19
Store

● 14
15   **Little**
●   **Pigeon**
            Church
Buckhorn Creek   ◆

16 ●   ● 20
      ◆ **Noah**
      Gordon's   ● 21
      Horse
      Mill   *to Ohio River and Hartford, Kentucky*

                                          ● 22

● 23   ● 24   ● 25

N

● 26

● 27   ● 28

Map: Andy Markley

	County Lines
	Township Lines
	Roads

121

Photograph courtesy of Young Abe Lincoln Muscial Outdoor Drama

"All that I am or hope to be, I owe to my angel mother."

APPENDIX B

INDIANA MEMORIALS TO ABRAHAM LINCOLN OPEN TO THE PUBLIC

LINCOLN BOYHOOD NATIONAL MEMORIAL

Tens of thousands of visitors each year enjoy the Lincoln Boyhood National Memorial at Lincoln City, Indiana, administered by the National Park Service of the U.S. Department of the Interior. The Visitor Center is open year round except Thanksgiving, Christmas, and New Year's Day. A twenty-four minute orientation film, *Here I Grew Up,* is shown on a regular basis. The Visitor Center includes a museum of Lincoln artifacts.

The Memorial complex includes the Lincoln Living Historical Farm, which is open daily from mid-April through October. It is a complete, working pioneer farmstead, including the log cabin, outbuildings, split rail fences, animals, gardens, and crop fields. Costumed "pioneers" present family living and farming activities. Visitors are encouraged to actually handle the tools, farm equipment, and even the clothing on display.

Lincoln Boyhood National Memorial

Lincoln Living Historical Farm

LINCOLN STATE PARK

The 1,747 acre Lincoln State Park adjoins the National Memorial, and it includes the Little Pigeon Creek Baptist Church with its cemetery where Lincoln's sister Sarah is buried. Park facilities include hiking trails; an 85 acre lake with boating, fishing, and swimming; picnic areas, family cabins, and a campground with electrical hookups and restrooms. The Park is open year round.

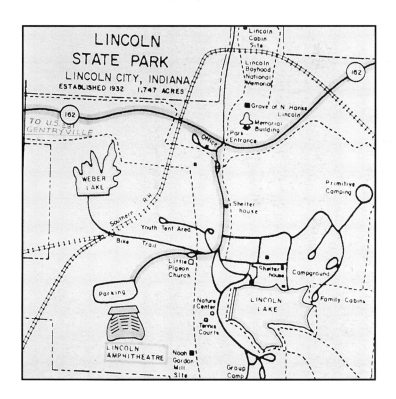

YOUNG ABE LINCOLN
MUSICAL OUTDOOR DRAMA

A musical outdoor drama on Lincoln's life in Indiana is presented during the summer in a modern amphitheater adjacent to the National Memorial. It is produced by the University of Southern Indiana for the Indiana Department of Natural Resources. The program begins nightly at 8:15 pm, except Mondays, late June through late August. It is under roof, eliminating rainouts. Preshow "Railsplitter Suppers" are available from 6 - 7:30 pm.

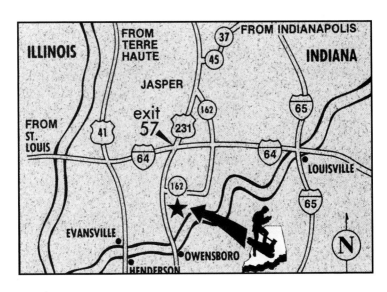

ACKNOWLEDGEMENTS

The author owes a great debt of gratitude to two Lincoln scholars, researchers, and historians who each spent a segment of their lives researching, in depth, the history of Abraham Lincoln's formative years in Indiana.

Francis Marion Van Natter spent 22 years researching Lincoln in Indiana. In his book *Lincoln's Boyhood - A Chronicle of his Indiana Years,* published in 1963 by Public Affairs Press, Washington, D.C., Van Natter has listed no fewer than 125 sources. Also, he conducted many personal interviews with descendants of Lincoln, his relatives, and his friends. Van Natter's research also included weeks of study at the greatest of all Lincolniana collections at the Lincoln National Life Foundation at Fort Wayne, Indiana, administered by Dr. Louis A. Warren (1885-1983).

Dr. Warren himself devoted 35 years — from 1928 to 1963 — researching the 14 years Lincoln lived in Indiana. His book, *Lincoln's Youth*, originally published in 1959 by the Indiana Historical Society, is the definitive work on the subject and includes over 250 sources. The book the reader holds in his hands could not have been written without the painstaking, meticulous research of these two dedicated Lincoln historians.

During the past half-century, renown artist Lloyd Ostendorf has produced over 225 drawings and photographs pertaining to Lincoln. He is the author of the splendid book, *Abraham Lincoln - The Boy • The Man.* I am deeply indebted to him for his gracious permission to reproduce many of his fine drawings and illustrations.

Photographs were made available by J.A. Benedict, Managing Director of the Young Abe Lincoln Outdoor Drama at Lincoln City, Indiana, who extended to me the opportunity to choose from hundreds of pictures in his files. The photograph on the back cover is from his collection.

The reproduction of the oil painting on canvas, *Boyhood of Lincoln* by Eastman Johnson (1824-1906), used on the front cover, is through the cooperation of Terry Kerby at the University of Michigan Museum of Art in Ann Arbor, Michigan.

Inez Hopkins of Evansville, Indiana, a student of Lincolniana, upon reading my previous books, felt that a book on Lincoln's life in Indiana, after the style of my other books, would be appropriate for my next literary effort. To bolster that contention, she sent me a copy of Dr. Warren's *Lincoln's Youth,* and I was soon engrossed in researching other works on the subject. This book is the result.

Few authors are fortunate enough to be married to a professional editor, but it is my good fortune to be in that position. My wife Betty not only edits my books in a superb fashion, but offers excellent suggestions for improving them as well.

INDEX

Note: page numbers in italics denote subject in illustration or caption.

INDEX

INDEX

ABOUT THE AUTHOR

W. Fred Conway, industrialist, historian, and author, served on the Board of Directors of the Lincoln Heritage Trail Foundation during the 1970's as one of two representatives from the state of Indiana. His desire to see Lincoln's youth in Indiana gain wider recognition has led to this, his fourth book in his series, "Books of Local Interest."

His area of local interest encompasses southern Indiana and northern Kentucky, which are bisected by the Ohio River. The first book in the series deals with the Battle of Corydon, one of only two official Civil War battles fought on northern soil. (The other one was Gettysburg.) His second book is a sequel, taking the flamboyant Confederate General John Hunt Morgan beyond Corydon to his capture, incredible prison escape, and death.

Next in his series is the adventures of Squire Boone, Daniel Boone's younger brother, whose exploits not only rivaled, but possibly surpassed those of his famous brother.

ABOUT THE AUTHOR

An avid fire buff, Fred Conway has authored the only book ever written on chemical fire engines, which for half a century (1872 - 1922) put out 80% of all fires in the United States. He maintains a museum of antique hand-drawn fire engines at the Conway Enterprises, Inc. manufacturing plant in the New Albany, Indiana, Industrial Park.

He is a graduate of Duke University with a degree in music and English. He and his wife Betty live in Floyds Knobs, Indiana.